THE *TENSES* IN ENGLISH LANGUAGE

M.A. SAMPSON

M.A.(Eng.Lit.), B.Ed., C.B.T.E.(Bhopal)

Himalaya Publishing House

ISO 9001:2015 CERTIFIED

First Edition : 2009
Edition : 2023
Edition : 2025

Published by : Mrs. Meena Pandey
for **Himalaya Publishing House Pvt. Ltd.,**
"Ramdoot", Dr. Bhalerao Marg, Girgaon, Mumbai - 400 004.
Phone: 022-23860170, 23863863; **Fax:** 022-23877178
E-mail: himpub@bharatmail.co.in; **Website:** www.himpub.com

Branch Offices :

New Delhi : "Pooja Apartments", 4-B, Murari Lal Street, Ansari Road, Darya Ganj, New Delhi - 110 002. Phone: 011-23270392, 23278631; Fax: 011-23256286

Nagpur : Kundanlal Chandak Industrial Estate, Ghat Road, Nagpur - 440 018. Mobile: 09325409992, 09325908881

Bengaluru : Plot No. 91-33, 2nd Main Road, Seshadripuram, Behind Nataraja Theatre, Bengaluru - 560 020. Phone: 080-41138821; Mobile: 09379847017, 09379847005

Hyderabad : No. 3-4-184, Lingampally, Besides Raghavendra Swamy Matham, Kachiguda, Hyderabad - 500 027. Phone: 040-27560041, 27550139

Chennai : No. 34/44, Motilal Street, T. Nagar, Chennai - 600 017. Mobile: 09380460419

Pune : "Laksha" Apartment, First Floor, No. 527, Mehunpura, Shaniwarpeth (Near Prabhat Theatre), Pune - 411 030. Phone: 020-24496323, 24496333; Mobile: 09370579333

Cuttack : Plot No 5F-755/4, Sector-9, CDA Markat Nagar, Cuttack - 753 014, Odisha. Mobile: 09338746007

Kolkata : 3, S.M. Bose Road, Near Gate No. 5, Agarpara Railway Station, North 24 Parganas, West Bengal - 700109. Mobile: 09674536325

DTP by : HPH, Editorial Office, Bhandup (Kalpana).

Printed at : Geetanjali Press Pvt. Ltd., Nagpur. On behalf of HPH (P).

Dedicated

to

the teachers

who constantly strive to make

learning

English Grammar

interesting,easy and effective.

M.A.S.

PREFACE TO SECOND EDITION

The author would like to express his deep gratitude to M/s K. N. Pandey, Anuj Pandey, Neeraj Pandey and Shri S. K. Patil of Himalaya Publications for showing their keen interest in the book and suggesting the change in the layout and other professional intricacies that go a long way in making the book attractive and readable. I also thank other staff of Himalaya Publication for their support in making the matter as flawless as possible and also making the cover page of the book attractive.

I hope the teachers who are willing to go an extra mile in helping the students enjoy learning **Tenses through Tense Tree Diagrams** by making it interesting which otherwise is feared to be dry and uninteresting subject.

I shall feel my efforts justified if both teachers and students find the book worth while.

Date: 16-03-2009

M. A. Sampson
71/119, New Collector Compound,
Malwani Colony, Malad (w.),
Mumbai - 4000 95
India

PREFACE

Depending on the time sense the Active Voice and Passive Voices are divided into three different main branches namely Indefinite Tenses, Continuous Tenses, and Perfect Tenses.

The First Section of the book deals with the Active Voice Tenses. ***A verb is in the Active Voice when its form shows that the person denoted by the Subject does something; or in other words, is the doer of the action.***

The branches **Indefinite, Continuous** and **Perfect** are further divided into three small branches depending on whether the action stated in the verb of the sentence does not pin point the exact time when it takes place(Indefiniteness): whether the action is still continuing at the given point at **present** time,**past** time or in the **future** time or whether the action is completed fully at the given point may it be in the ***present time, past time*** or in the ***future time***

The figure of the Active Voice Tense tree gives,at glance, the ***scope of the tenses*** it has in it.Each branch has seven personal pronouns and they are grouped under the appropriate verb that they take.The verb form is given on the leaf of the branch at the end. If the verb has any additional verbs like modal and helping verbs they are given on the **placards** (board) hung to the branch at the appropriate place.

This Visual Aid in learning English grammar helps increase accuracy of formation of finite verb to be used in the sentences dealing with the particular tense situation.

*The verb '**to see**' is purposely chosen to conjugate in all the tenses as its verb has four different forms and can be easily recognised easily unlike if the verb like 'to love' which has same form of past and past participle.*

Invariably the sentences of present indefinite and present continuous are confused with each other.

I go to market and ***I am going to market*** do not mean the same.First sentence should mean going to market everyday and the second sentence means that the subject is actually in the process of going to the market. I have the book and I am having the book do not,also, mean exactly the same thing, The first states the possession of the book ***at present but for indefinite time*** and second sentence states possession is ***still to take place*** and it is in the process. (Possession is not complete.) Hence sometimes this tense is also called as incomplete tense in the place of continuous tense.

Rest of the attributes are discussed in details in the following pages.

Date: 12, February 2007

71/119, New Collector Compound,
Malwani Colony, Malad (w.),
Mumbai - 4000 95
India

INTRODUCTION

Enthusiasm with which his former editions '*The complete book of English Grammar Through Diagrams*' and '*Articles - A Peculiarity in English Language*' has been received has compelled Mr. Sampson to bring out this edition of 'Tenses'. He hopes and believes that the book will now have an approval and cater to the needs of the students.

'Some teaching aid is better than no teaching aid at all' for teaching English Grammar is what Mr. Sampson believes in. Keeping this in mind he set about publishing a book on the Tenses in English Language which will enable the students to learn and remember ***how to convert*** Active Voice into Passive Voice and vice versa.

Accuracy in writing or speaking increases by learning Tenses through ***tree diagrams, the*** **first of its kind** in the study of English Grammar. He has made it so easy and interesting that with the help of this technique one can master the tenses easily.

Mr. Sampson believes in *'No gains without pains'* and had he not learned **CorelDraw** himself for producing tree diagrams for the book to simplify learning tenses, this book would not have been a reality. This makes the work more helpful to the students and leaves a lasting impression on the minds of the learner. ***No pains have been spared to keep the book well ahead of similar publication*** in regard to the ***simplicity***, ***correctness*** and ***elegance*** of Language and its general usefulness. The book is designed in such a way the students and teachers will,both, be benefitted.

Sd/-

Date: 12, February 2007

Mrs. A. K. Amrolia

Former Incharge Head,
Department of English,
S.B.M.Polytechnic
Vile Parle,Mumbai-400 56

ACKNOWLEDGEMENTS

The author extends his sincere thanks to :

Mrs. A. K. Amrolia who has gone through the book and has written an introduction to the book.She was an Incharge head of English Department in Shri Bhagubhai Mafatlal Polytechnic at Vile Parle Mumbai -56.She has a Master's Degree in English from Mumbai University and also earned a gold medal for her master's Degree in History from Karnatak University. I am thankful for her sincere opinion that the book will be useful for both teachers as well as students.

My sincere thanks to **Mr. K.R.Amrolia** for his appreciation of not only this book but also all the ventures I have undertaken to make English learning easy,interesting and effective.He opines that 'Logical approach of the book in learning and teaching will be beneficial to anyone one who cares to put across his thoughts accurately.'

I am thankful to my friend **Mr. Kamalakar Hari Juvekar** who is actually using this approach of my book in teaching active voice sentences to Students who undergo his courses in English speaking. He is very particular about the accuracy of tenses in speaking English special competency to be achieved by any vernacular students.

For guidance in preparing master tree diagram in initial stages I extend my heartfelt thanks to **Mr. Deepak Harwande** (G.D.Art) which encouraged me to learn and accomplish this difficult task of presenting tenses through tree branches to make it easier to learn and teach tenses in English Language.I would like to record my thanks in advance to the following people for their promise to translate this book in other vernacular languages:

1. **Mr. H. Vijay Bhasker -** for Kannada Language

2. **Mrs. Shakila Sanaullah Khan** for Urdu Translation

3. **Mr. Satish Kumar Sampson** for Hindi Translation.

CONTENTS

Section-3

Branch that Does not have Passive Equivalent

❒ ❒ ❒

Section - 1
Active Voice

SHORT FORMS

to be:	am, is , are, was, were
M:	Modal Verbs like will should etc.
NP:	Negative Particle 'no' and 'not'
S:	Subject or Subject Phrase
O:	Object or Object Phrase
V:	Present Tense form of the verb like go, write etc.
Vs:	Present tense form 's' added to it belonging to third person, singular number and present tense e.g. writes, does, goes, is,has etc.
Ving:	Present Participle form of the verb like writing, coming, bringing etc.
Ved:	Past Tense form of the verb like wrote, sang, pulled, brought etc.
Ven:	Past participle form of the verb like written, sung, brought, pulled etc.
T:	Time Phrase
All Persons:	I,we,;you;he,she,It,they

TENSE TREE - ACTIVE VOICE

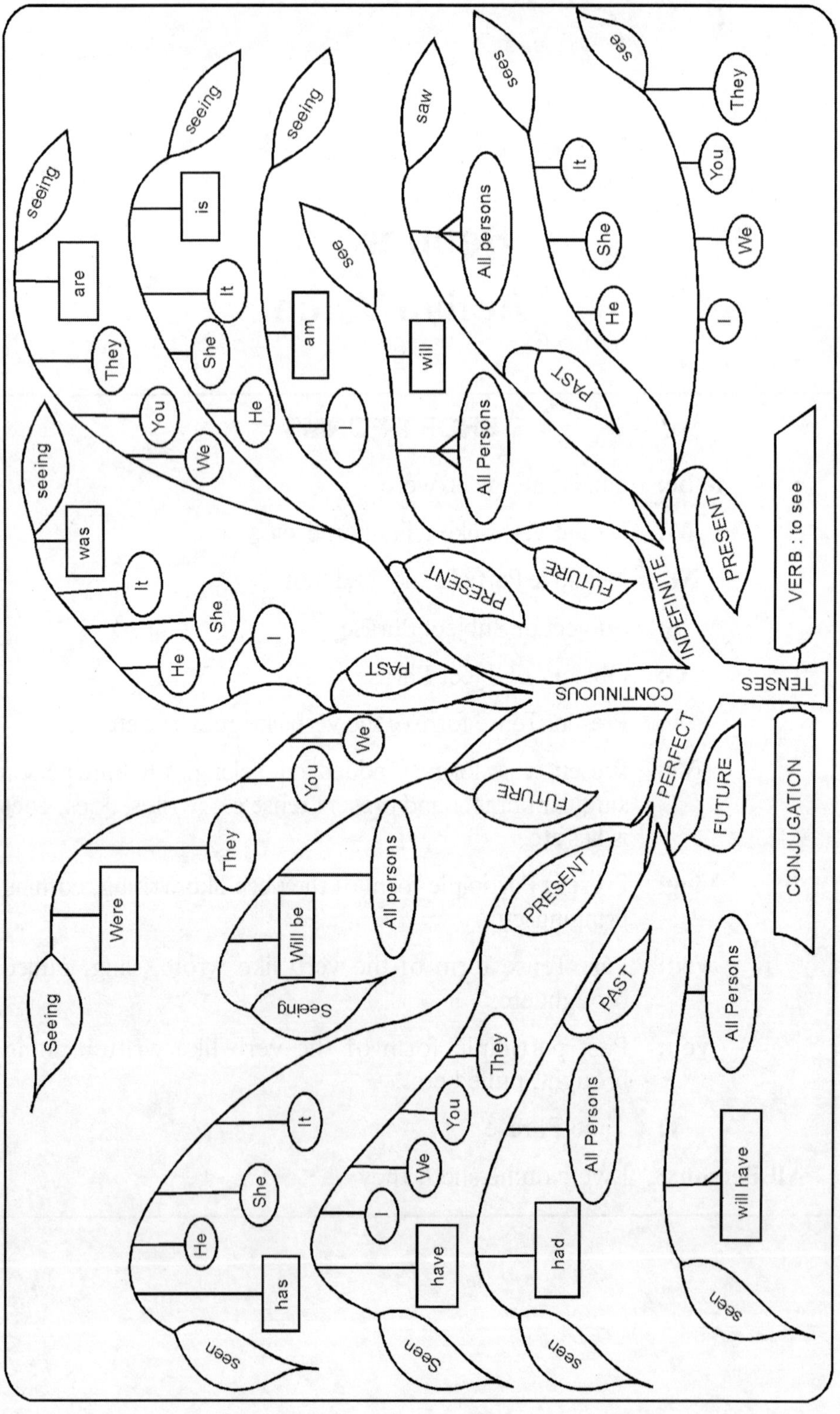

ACTIVE VOICE TREE

Tenses are represented by the full tree known as 'Tense Tree' in ***Indicative Mood for affirmative sentences***. Assertive sentence in Negative, Interrogative Positive and Interrogative Negative sentences are given in the text following Affirmative of Assertive sentence. Short form structures of Assertive Negative and Interrogative Negative are given after that.***Short forms used in the structures*** are given at the beginning of the each section and also on some other pages for convenient and ready reference..

This tree which gives conjugation of the verb 'to see' in indicative mood, has three main branches representing ***Indefinite, Continuous*** and ***Perfect Tenses.*** These main branches are further divided into three small branches each representing time. Based on the time the main branches are divided into ***present tense, past tense*** and ***future tenses.***To the small branches are hung fruits looking like apples. Each apple represents a *personal pronoun.*Three leaves are to show present tense branch past tense branch and the future tense branch.Leaves at the end of each small branch are of the required form of a ***main verb***. In this tree it is the verb 'to see'.Wherever there is need of either the simple ***auxiliary*** verb or a ***modal*** verb it is written on a placard or a small board and is hung to the small branch to which it belongs.

All this figurative representation is an effort ***to make learning tenses effective, easy to remember and to make the whole process of learning Tenses very interesting.***

This representation also lets the learner ***know the scope*** of learning tenses beforehand which makes him prepare himself to sustain his effort towards completing the task of mastering them.

The structure of the book is an extension of tense tree format. Though only Assertive Affirmative structures are shown by the tree, the study of the tenses for meaningul communication involves in formation of Assertive Negative sentences, Interrogative Positive sentences, and Interrogative Negative sentences and also the sentences with Short forms of modal verbs with Negative Particle are described in details following their full forms.

If, mastery in indicative and interrogative mood sentences is achieved the other mood sentences like ***Imperative*** and ***Subjunctive*** will not pose as much complication as indicative and interrogative mood sentences. Hence the Assertive and Interrogative sentences have been dealt in details.

_______Author

Active Voice

Indefinite Tense Branch

Present	Past	Future

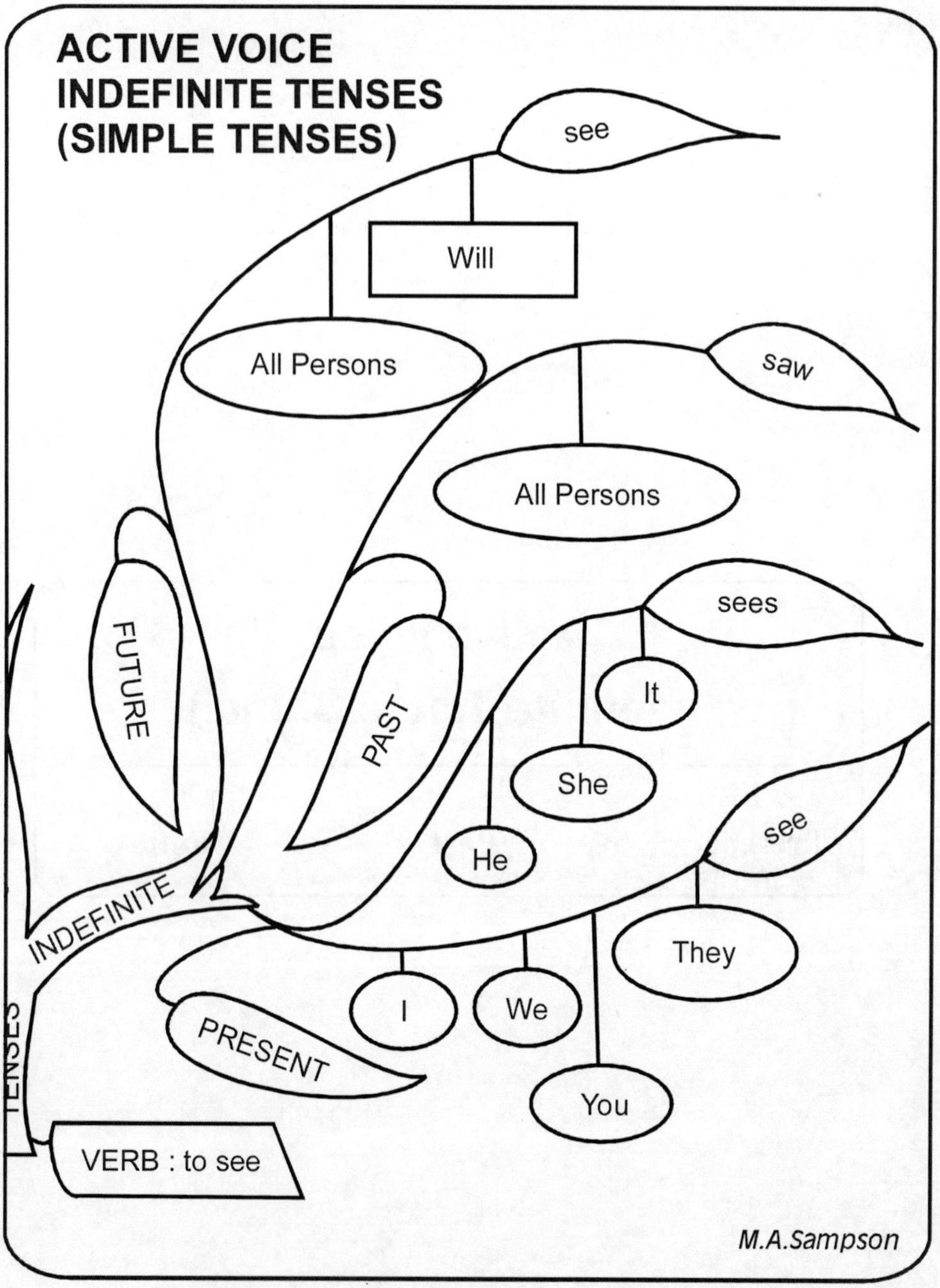

(Active Voice Indefinite Tense Branch showing letters to all the branches)

Active Voice
Indefinite Tense Branch

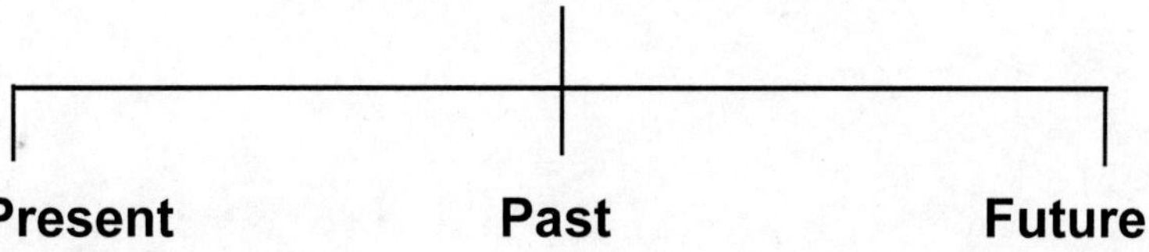

Tenses denote the *time of Action*. The tense of a verb indicates the *time* expressed by it.

The part of Speech that is chiefly concerned with the passage of time is the Verb. So the verb has many tenses. A verb may refer to

(1) Present time

(2) Past time and

(3) Future time

1. Present Tense:

A Verb that refers to *present time* or *habitual action* is said to be in the Present Tense.

For example: (a) I give. (b) I play. (c) I sing.

2. Past Tense:

A Verb that refers to the *past time* or action completed in the past is said to be in the **Past Tense**. This tense denotes *events, actions* and *situation* which occurred in the past and are now finished.

For example: (a) I gave. (b) I played. (c) I sang.

3. Future Tense:

A Verb that refers to future time or action to be done in the future is said to be in the Future Tense.

For example: *(a) I shall give. (b) I will play. (c) I will see.*

❐ ❐ ❐

SHORT FORMS

to be:	am, is , are, was, were
M:	Modal Verbs like will should etc.
NP:	Negative Particle 'no' and 'not'
S:	Subject or Subject Phrase
O:	Object or Object Phrase
V:	Present Tense form of the verb like go, write etc.
Vs:	Present tense form 's' added to it belonging to third person, singular number and present tense e.g. writes, does, goes, is,has etc.
Ving:	Present Participle form of the verb like writing, coming, bringing etc.
Ved:	Past Tense form of the verb like wrote, sang, pulled, brought etc.
Ven:	Past participle form of the verb like written, sung, brought, pulled etc.
T:	Time Phrase
All Persons:	I,we,;you;he,she,It,they

Active Voice
Present Indefinite Tense

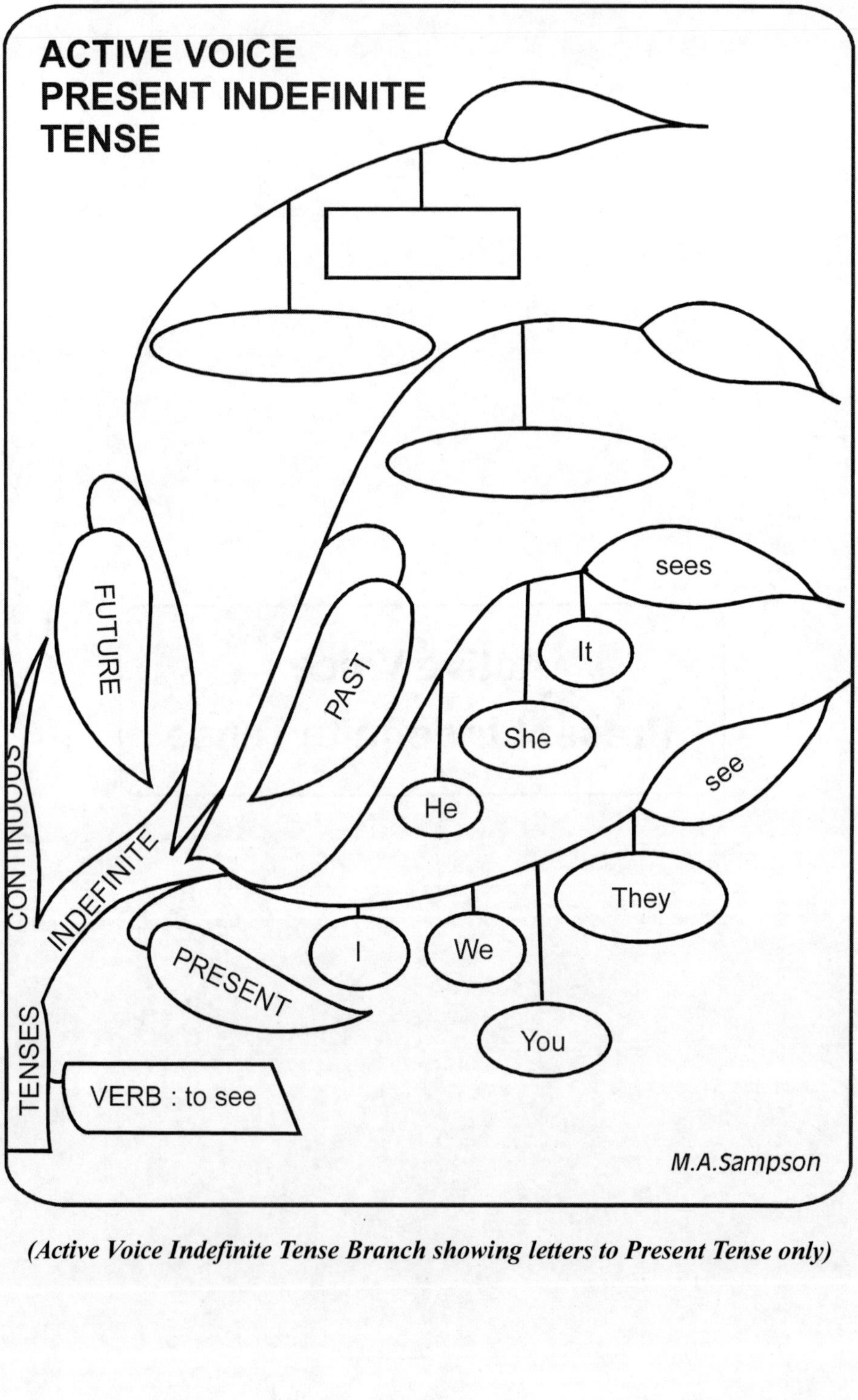

(Active Voice Indefinite Tense Branch showing letters to Present Tense only)

Present Indefinite Tense

Assertive Affirmative

Form: **Subject + V / Vs + Object + T.**
All Persons + write/writes+ a letter + everyday

e.g. (1) *We + play + cricket + everyday.*
Subject + V + Object + T.

(2) *You + play + cricket + everyday.*
Subject + V + Object +T.

(3) *They + get up + everyday at 6 O'clock.*
Subject + V + T.

(4) *He + writes + a letter + once in a while.*
Subject + Vs + Object + T.

(5) *She + dances + well.*
Subject + Vs + Adv.

(6) It + *dances + well.*
Subject + Vs + Adv.

In sentences, the Verbs i.e. *writes, play, get up, dances, etc.* simply express the *action* done in the present time, *without* indicating the state of action. It does not tell us anything about the *completeness or incompleteness* of the action. Hence the Verb is said to be in present Indefinite or ***Simple Present Tense.***

In Simple Present Tense, when the subject is ***of Singular number and of third person(He, She , It)*** , add the letter *'s'* or 'es' to the verb root and change 'have' to 'has' form and the verb ending in y is changed into ies.

e.g.

a. I eat.		a. He *eats*
b. You eat.	but	b. She *eats*
c. We eat.		c. It eat*s*.
d. I *have* a book.		d. She *has* a book.
e. I carry my bag.		e. He *caries* his bag.
f. They catch fish.		f. He catches fish.

Assertive Negative

Form: **Subject + M + NP + V + Object + T.**
All Persons + do/does + not + write + a letter + everyday.

e.g. (1) *He + does+ not+write + a letter.*+**everyday.**
S +M + NP + V + Object + T.

(2) *We +do+not + play + cricket + everyday.*
S + M + NP + V + Object + T.

(3) *They + do+not+get up + everyday at 6 O'clock.*
S + M + NP + V + T.

(4) *She + does +not + dance + well.*
S + M + NP + V + Adv.

Interrogative Positive

Form: **M + Subject + V + Object + T + ?**

Do/Does + he + write + a letter + everyday+ ?.

e.g. (1) *Does+he + write + a letter + everyday +?.*
M + S + V + Object + T + ?

(2) *Do+we + play + cricket + everyday+ ?.*
M + S + V +Object + T + ?

(3) *Do+they + get up + everyday at 6 O'clock+?.*
M + S + V + T + ?

(4) *Does +she + dance + well +?.*
M + S + V + Adv. + ?

Interrogative Negative

Form: **M + Subject + NP + V + Object + T +?**

Do/ Does + All Persons + not + write+ a letter +everyday+?

e.g. (1) *Does+he +not+ write + a letter everyday+?*
M + S + NP + V + Object + T + ?

(2) *Do+we +not+ play + cricket everyday + ?*
M + S + NP + V + Object + T + ?

(3) Do+*they +not+ get up + everyday at 6 O'clock+?*
M + S + NP + V + T +?

(4) *Does+she + not + dance + well+ ?*
M + S + NP + V + Adv. +?

SHORT FORMS

Assertive Negative

***Form*:Subject + M+NP + V +Object + T**

He + Doesn't + write +a letter+ everyday.

e.g.(1) *He+ doesn't + write + a letter.*

S + M+NP + V + Object .

(2) *We + don't + play + cricket+ everyday.*

S +M+NP + V + Object + T

(3) *They+don't + get up + everyday at 6 O'clock.*

S +M+NP + V + T

(4) *She + doesn't+ dance+ well .*

S + M+NP + V + Adv.

Interrogative Negative

***Form*: M+NP +Subject + V + Object + T + ?**

Doesn't + he + write + a letter+everyday+?

e.g.(1) *Doesn't + he + write + a letter+ ?*

M+NP + S + V +Object + ?

(2) *Don't + we + play + cricket+ everyday+ ?*

M+NP + S + V + Object + T + ?

(3) *Don't + they + get up + everyday at 6 'clock+?*

M+NP + S + V + T + ?

(4) *Doen't + she + dance+ well +?*

M+NP + S + V + Adv..+?

SIMPLE PRESENT TENSE IS USED:

1. To express regular or habitual actions:

I ***get up*** *early and* ***eat*** *my breakfast.*

We can be more precise about habitual actions by using the Simple Present with Adverbs of Frequency such as *always, ever, never, occasionally,* or with Adverbial Phrases like *every day, twice a month on Sundays. etc.*

(a) I *go* for a walk *every evening.*

(b) The Minister *reads* the newspaper *everyday after breakfast.*

(c) We *go* to Church *twice a week.*

(d) He *comes* here *twice every month.*

(e) I *practise* speaking English *everyday.*

2. To express the Neutral present. This is used when no particular time is thought of : as

This tense is used to refer to events, actions and situations which are true at the time of speaking and which may continue indefinitely as

(a) The earth *moves* round the sun.

(b) Dogs *make better* pets than cats.

(c) Horses *do* not see colours.

(d) My father *works* in an office.

(e) Our school *has* a big hall.

3. To express a universal truth.

(a) Honey *is* sweet.

(b) Light *is faster* than sound.

(c) The sun *rises* in the east and *sets* in the west.

(d) A chemical reaction *takes place* in the fuel cell.

❒ ❒ ❒

Active Voice
Past Indefinite Tense
or
Past Simple

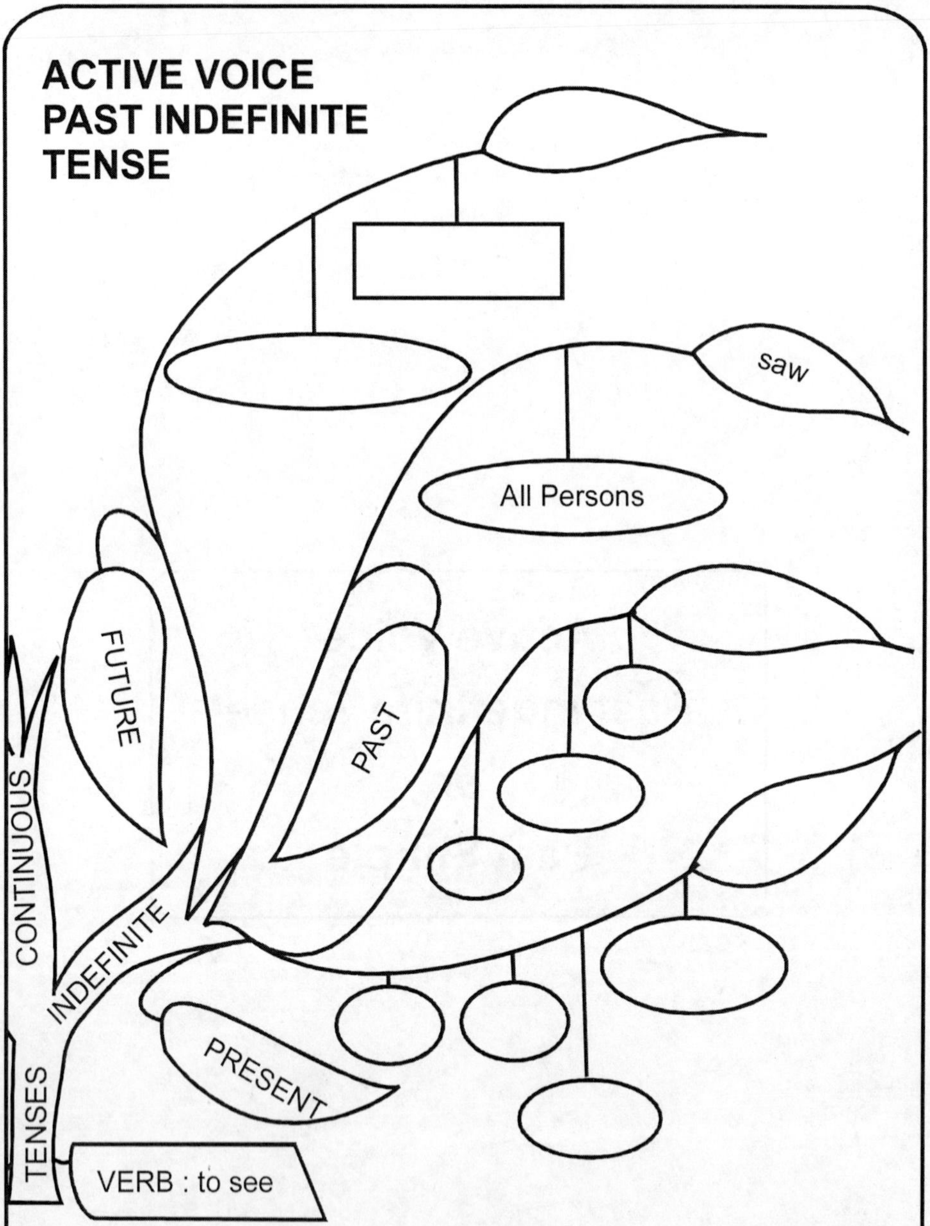

(Active Voice Indefinite Tense Branch showing letters to Past Tense only)

Past Indefinite Tense

Assertive Affirmatives

Form: Subject + Ved + Object + T.

All Persons + wrote + a letter + yesterday.

e.g. (a) He + wrote + a letter + yesterday.

(b) They + played + football + long ago.

In the past simple, the verb shows that the event was completed at a point of times in the past and thus it is separated from the present.

(a) I wrote a letter.

(b) We wrote a letter.

(c) You wrote a letter.

(d) He wrote a letter.

(e) She wrote a letter.

(f) It wrote a letter.

(g) They wrote a letter.

From the above sentences, it can be seen that the past tense verb form is used for all the personal pronouns.

Assertive Negative

***Form:* Subject + M + NP + V +Object + T.**
All Persons + did+not+write + a letter + yesterday.

e.g. (a) He + did + not + write + a letter + yesterday.

(b) They + did + not + play + football + long ago.

Interrogative Positive

***Form:* M + Subject + V + Object + T + ?**
Did + All Persons + write + a letter + yesterday +?

e.g. (a) Did + he + write + a letter + yesterday + ?

(b) Did + they + play + football + long ago + ?

Interrogative Negative

Form: **M + Subject + NP + V + Object + T + ?**
Did + All Persons + not +write + a letter + yesterday + ?

e.g. (a) Did + he + not + write + a letter + yesterday + ?.

(b) Did + they + not + play + football + long ago + ?

SHORT FORMS

Note the following short forms of the modal verb with negative particle 'not'.

Assertive Negative

Form: **Subject + M + NP + V + Object + T.**

All Persons + didn't + write + a letter + yesterday.

e.g. (a) He + didn't + write + a letter + yesterday.

(b) They + didn't + play + football + long ago.

Note the short form 'Didn't'of the modal verb with negative particle'not'could be used

When this short form is used it comes after the subject in assertive negative sentences

Interrogative Negative

Form: **M+NP+ Subject + V + Object + T + ?**

Didn't + All Persons+ write+ a letter + yesterday + ?

e.g. (a) Didn't + he + write + a letter + yesterday + ?

(b) Didn't + they + play+football + long ago + ?

Note the short form 'Didn't'of the modal verb with negative particle'not'comes before the subject while other form of the sentence structure remains the same.v

Rules

THE SIMPLE PAST TENSE IS USED AS:

(a) An action that took place and completed at a point of time in the past or for a past action if the time of that action is given.

(1) She went home.

(2) They saw a picture.

(3) It rained yesterday.

(4) She left our house only an hour ago.

(b) Sometimes past continuous can also be expressed in past simple tense.

He played (i.e. was playing) while I watched (i.e. was watching).

In this case, it means that the use of simple past tense is made instead of past continuous tense.

(c) To express habitual or regular actions in the past: If we want to talk about an activity that took place regularly or repeatedly in the past, but which no longer occurs, we use the Simple Past: as

(a) He took tea daily.

(b) We played a great deal in my School days.

(c) On Sundays, we trekked to the holidays home.

(d) Sometimes simple past is used without an Adverb of time. In such cases, the time may be either implied or indicated by the context.

(1) I learned English in England.

(2) She didn't sleep well.

(3) We defeated them.

(e) To express an action which occurred in a period of time in the past.

(1) The teacher laughed, but the boys fooled.

(2) The mother wept with her dead child on her lap.

(3) In the depth of the forest, the lion roared.

(f) When the person speaking wants to find out the time of the action; as

(1) When did you come?

(2) When did you see her?

(g) When the action took place at a definite time but this time is not mentioned explicitly; as

(1) The train arrived four hours late. (which (four hours) is not mentioned.

(2) I bought this pen in Paris.

(h) To denote past situation: This tense is used to denote a situation which existed over a period of time in the past; as

(1) He lived in Calcutta during his childhood.

(2) Throughout 1997, he studied French at School.

If you are talking about something that happened in the past and you mention a situation that existed at that time, you use the Simple Past. You can do this whether or not the situation still exists; as,

(a) In the centre of the village there was one of India's most famous temples.

(b) All buildings in this part of Lucknow looked alike

(i) In polite enquiries

The Simple Past can also be used with polite enquiries often with verbs like *hope, think* or *wonder*; as

(a) I wonder if you would *lend me that book.*

(b) I hope he would *excuse me.*

Rule 1: If there is a Past tense in the Principal Clause, it must be followed by a Past tense in the Subordinate Clause, as

1. *I knew that he wanted to go home.*
2. *I would do this if I were allowed.*

Rule 2: A Present or Future Tense in the Principal Clause may be followed by any tense required by the sense in the subordinate Clause as -

1. *I think that the picture is beautiful.*
2. *You will learn that she works hard.*
3. *He will say that she will work well.*

Rule 3: A Past Tense in the Principal Clause may be followed by a Present Tense in the Subordinate Clause when the subordinate clause expresses some habitual or universal fact; as

1. *The teacher taught us that the earth is round.*
2. *The King said that all men are mortal.*
3. *Galileo proved that the earth moves round the sun.*

Rule 4: When the Subordinate Clause is introduced by the Conjunction of Comparison "than" Rule does not apply at all. Any tense can be followed by any tense; as

1. *She likes you better than she liked me.*
2. *She liked you better than she likes me. etc.*

Note: If the comparison is expressed by as well as instead of than, the same rule holds good. Any tense may be followed by any tense, according the sense intended by the speaker.

1. *She likes me as well as she liked.*
2. *She will like me as well as she liked him.*

Exercise-1

Fill in the blanks with correct form of the verbs given in the brackets to give sense of appropriate tense:

1. I realised that I _____ (take) the wrong decision.
2. She _____ (leave) by the time Mohan arrived.
3. She said that she ______ (see) that movie.
4. He said that he ______ (complete) the poem.
5. He said that he ______ (see) the culprit before.
6. He asked me why I _____ (leave) the party so early.
7. He knew that he ______ (make) a serious mistake.
8. Previously she ______ (be) a very promising candidate.
9. By the time we arrived they _____ (go).
10. It was reported that the police _____ (capture) the culprit.

❐ ❐ ❐

SHORT FORMS

to be:	am, is , are, was, were
M:	Modal Verbs like will should etc.
NP:	Negative Particle 'no' and 'not'
S:	Subject or Subject Phrase
O:	Object or Object Phrase
V:	Present Tense form of the verb like go, write etc.
Vs:	Present tense form 's' added to it belonging to third person, singular number and present tense e.g. writes, does, goes, is, has etc.
Ving:	Present Participle form of the verb like writing, coming, bringing etc.
Ven:	Past participle form of the verb like written, sung, brought, pulled etc.
T:	Time Phrase
All Persons:	I,we,;you;he,she,It,they

Active Voice
Future Indefinite Tense
(Simple Tense)

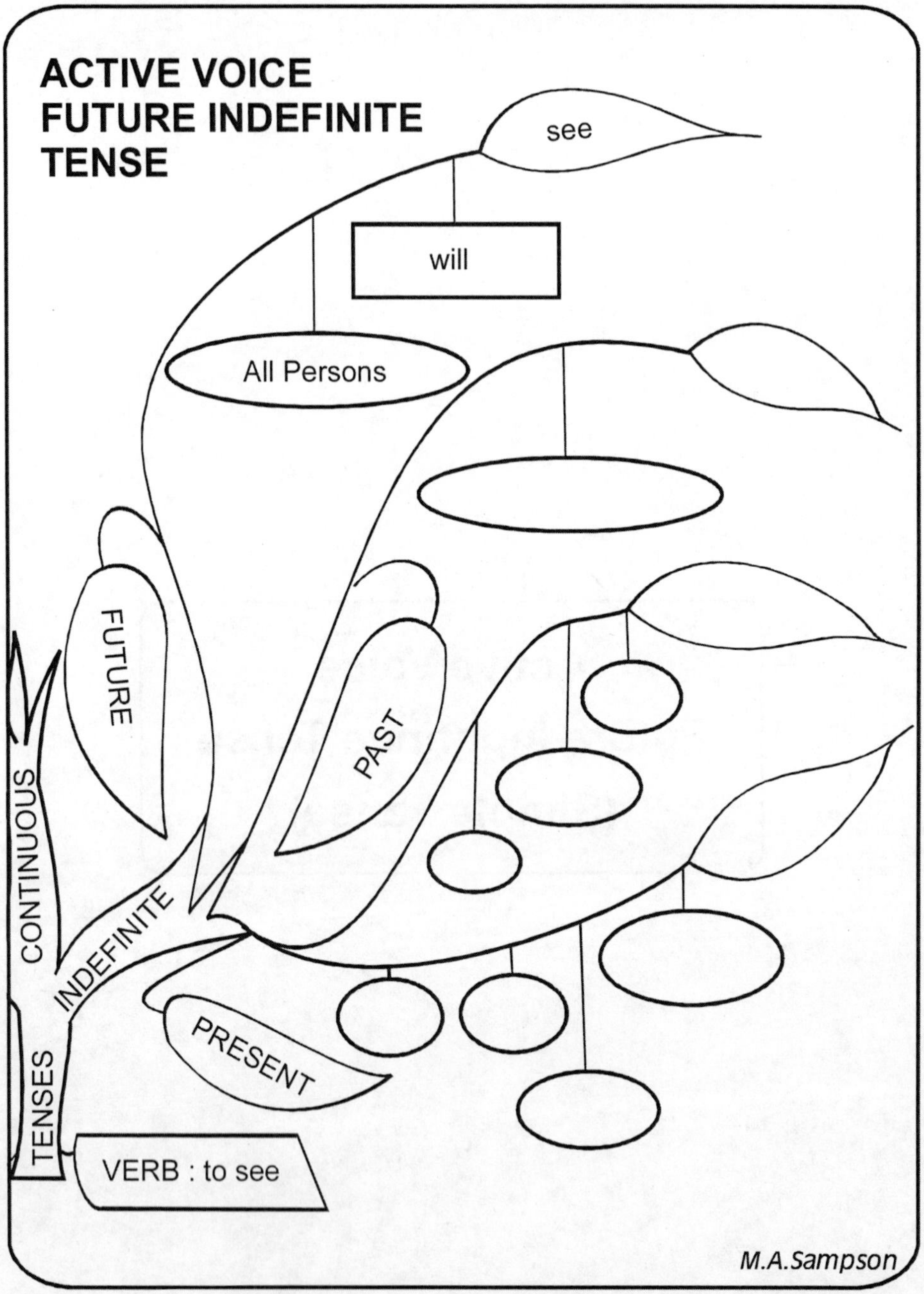

(Active Voice Indefinite Tense Branch showing letters to Future Tense only)

Simple Future Tense

Assertive Affirmative

Form: Subject + M + V + Object + T.
First Person + shall + write + a letter + tomorrow.

e.g. I + shall + sing + a song+ tomorrow +in the auditorium.

We + shall + sing + a song + tomorrow in the auditorium.

Form: Subject + M + V +Object + T.
Second and third persons + will + write + a letter+ tomorrow.

e.g. You + will + sing + a song + before a large audience tomorrow

She + will + sing + a song+before students tomorrow

He + will + sing + a song+before students tomorrow.

They + will + sing + before students tomorrow.

Assertive Negative

***Form*: Subject + M + NP + V + Object + T.**
First Person+ Shall + not + write + a letter + tomorrow.

e.g. I + shall +not- sing + a song+ tomorrow +in the auditorium.

We + shall + sing + a song + tomorrow in the auditorium.

***Form:* Subject + M + NP + V + Object + T.**
Second and Third person + will + not + write + a letter. + tomorrow

e.g. You +will+ sing+ a song+ before a large audience tomorrow

She + will + sing + a song+before students tomorrow

He + will + sing + a song+before students tomorrow.

They + will + sing + before students tomorrow.

Interrogative Positive

***Form*: M + First Person + V + Object + T + ?**
Shall + I / we + write + a letter + tomorrow +?

e.g. Shall + I + sing + a song+ tomorrow + in the auditorium?

Shall + we + sing + a song + tomorrow in the auditorium?

***Form*: M + Second/Third persons+V + Object + T + ?**

Will + you/he/she/It/they + write + a letter + tomorrow + ?

e.g. Will + you + sing + a song + before a large audience tomorrow?

Will + she/he + sing + a song + before studentstomorrow?

Will + they + sing + before students tomorrow?

Interrogative Negative

***Form:* M + First Person+ NP + V + Object + T + ?**

Shall + I / we + not +write + a letter +tomorrow + ?

e.g. Shall + I/we +not + sing + a song+ tomorrow +in the auditorium+?

Form: M + Second/Third persons+NP + V +Object + T + ?

Will + you/he/she/It/they +not+write+a letter+ tomorrow+?

e.g. Will +you+not + sing + a song + before a large audience tomorrow+?

SHORT FORMS

Note the following short forms of the modal verb with negative particle 'not'.

Assertive Negative

***Form:* First Person + M+ NP + V + Object + T.**

I/We + Shan't + write + a letter + tomorrow.

Second / Third person + M+NP + V + Object + T.

You/He/She/It/They + won't + write + a letter. + tomorrow.

Interrogative Negative

***Form*: M + NP + First Person + V + Object + T + ?**

Shan't +I/we+sing +a song+tomorrow in the auditorium +?

e.g. *Shan't* +they + sing + before students tomorrow+?

***Form*: M + NP + Second/Third persons + V + Object +T+ ?**

Won"t + he/she/it/they + sing + a song + before students tomorrow+?

e.g. *Won"t*+you + sing+ a song+ before a large audience tomorrow + ?

Won"t+ she +sing + a song+before students tomorrow + ?

Won"t+ he + sing + a song+before students tomorrow + ?

Won"t+they + sing + before students tomorrow + ?

THE SIMPLE FUTURE IS USED:

A. to express actions in the future i.e. action that has still to take place.

1. *I shall meet you tomorrow.*
2. *The doctor will examine the patients in the evening.*
3. *They will arrive soon.*

B. to express habitual action in the future.

1. *The rainy season will come.*
2. *My son will run this firm exactly as I am doing now.*

C. To express the speaker's opinions or assumptions about the future. Verbs such as think, believe, expect, hope, suppose etc. introduce such opinions.

e.g. 1. *I suppose they will bring enough food for all.*

2. *I expect he will do better next time.*
3. *Do you think she will come back?*

D. To predict what we think will happen; as

1. *The festival will last for a week.*
2. *One day, people will travel to Mars.*
3. *We will win the match.*

E. To indicate an offer or a promise; as

1. *I shall post that letter for you.*
2. *I will give you a gift, if you pass.*

F. To indicate an instant decision (at the moment of speaking);

(1) *It is very hot. I will put on the fan.*

(2) *It is my birthday. We will have a party.*

G. After verbs and verb phrases like be sure, think, expect, suppose, hope, believe, etc.; as

(1) *I hope he will come tomorrow.*

(2) *I'm sure it will be all right.*

(3) *I expect we will win the match.*

Note 1: You can express the future in other ways as shown below:

Be going to : We are going to win the match.

Be to: He is to see the Headmaster tomorrow.

Present Continuous: He is seeing the Headmaster tomorrow.

Simple Present: He sees the Headmaster tomorrow.

Note 2: We use to (and not will) to express an intention:

Amit and Anita are planning something very exciting. They are going ***to sail*** *round the world.*

Note:3 The first person "I" and second person "You" are the use of *Simple Present Tense:*

Exercise 1

Complete the following sentences with the 'will' future form of the verbs given in brackets:

1. I ________ (buy) a shirt for you.
2. Ravi ______ (do) that job well in time.
3. She ______ (sing) a song for you.
4. I ______ (leave) the country soon.
5. We ______ (see) you on next Sunday.
6. The shops _______ (close) at 7.30 p.m. tomorrow.
7. Rita _______ (wash) the curtains after an hour.

❒ ❒ ❒

Active Voice
Continuous Branch

Present | Past | Future

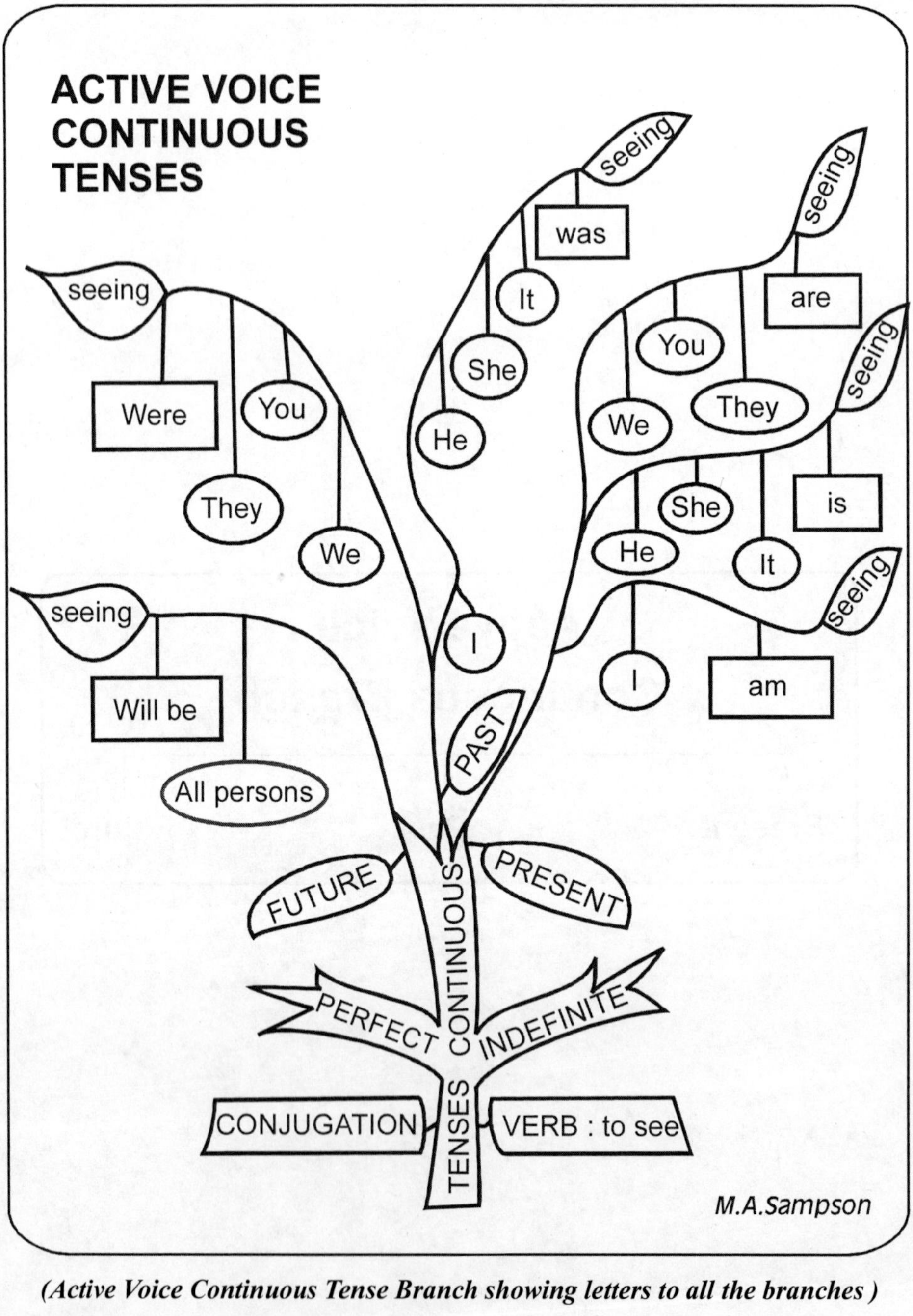

(Active Voice Continuous Tense Branch showing letters to all the branches)

Active Voice

Continuous Branch

This branch (tense) is always confused with the indefinite branch,. specially the present tenses are confused with their indefiniteness and continuousness.. Hence if the continuous branch is properly studied there should be no reason why we should get confused while using these tenses either in talking or in writing. The tense tree will help you differentiate these tenses.

Present

Form: **Subject + Present tobe + Ving + Object + Time.**

e.g. : I + am + seeing + a film + now.

He,She, It, + is + writing + a letter . + now.

You, We, They + are + sleeping + now.

Past

Form: **Subject + past to be + Ving + Object + Time.**

I, He,She,It + was + writing + a letter +when I saw him.

We,You,They+were + digging + a hole + when I saw them.

Future

Form: **Subject + M + be + Ving + Object + Time.**

I + shall + be + writing + a letter + tomorrow at 9 p.m.

She + will + be + singing + a song + tomorrow at 9 p.m.

They + will + be + digging + a hole + tomorrow at 9 p.m.

(Details about these tenses are under the respective branches)

❒ ❒ ❒

SHORT FORMS

to be:	am, is , are, was, were
M:	Modal Verbs like will should etc.
NP:	Negative Particle 'no' and 'not'
S:	Subject or Subject Phrase
O:	Object or Object Phrase
V:	Present Tense form of the verb like go, write etc.
Vs:	Present tense form 's' added to it belonging to third person, singular number and present tense e.g. writes, does, goes, is, has etc.
Ving:	Present Participle form of the verb like writing, coming, bringing etc.
Ven:	Past participle form of the verb like written, sung, brought, pulled etc.
T:	Time Phrase
All Persons:	I,we,;you;he,she,It,they

Active Voice
Present Continuous Tense

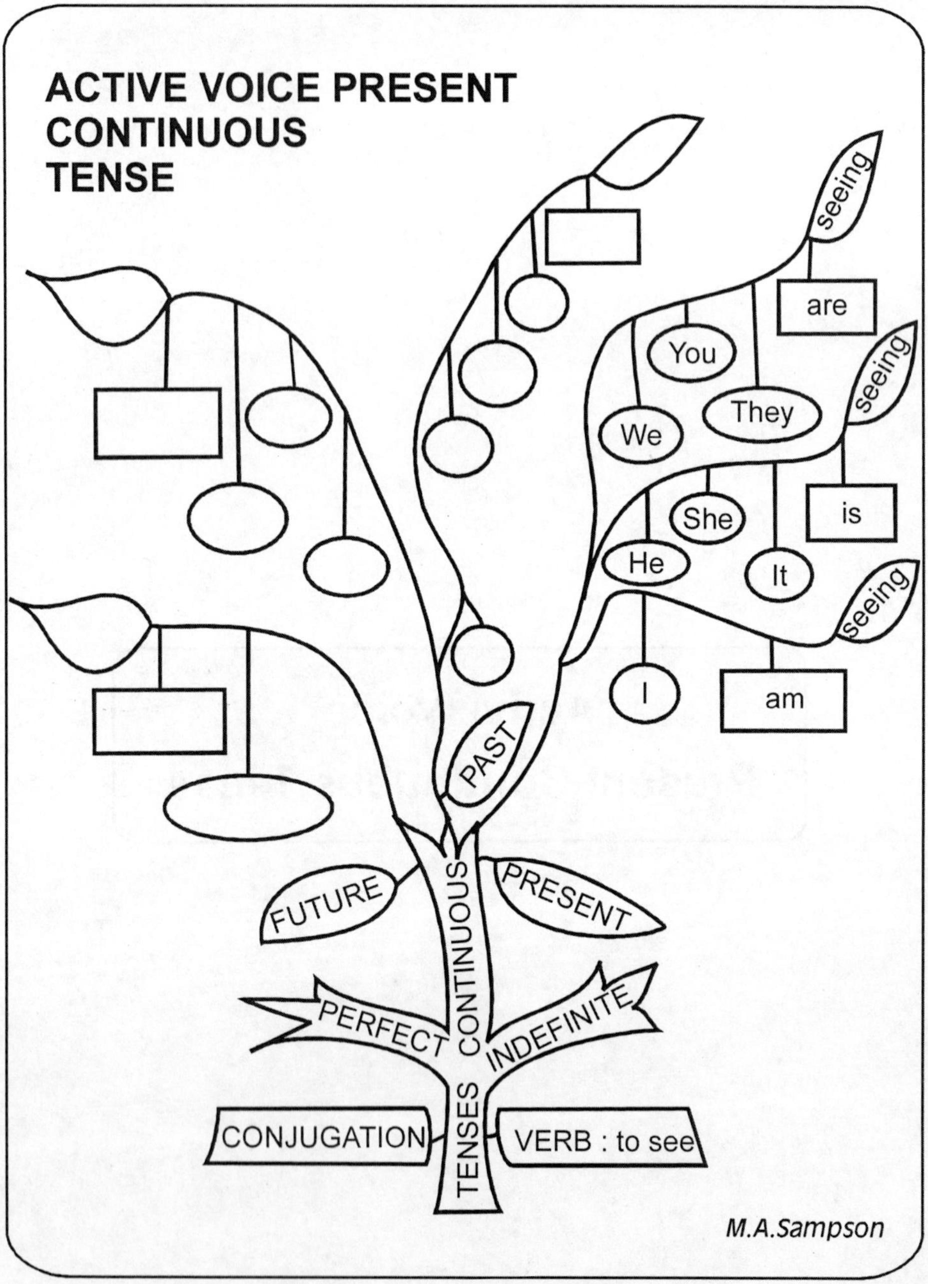

(Active Voice Continuous Tense Branch showing letters to Present Tense only)

Present Continuous Tense

Assertive Affirmative

Form: **Subject + Am/Is/Are + Ving + Object + Time.**

e.g. : I + am + seeing + a film + now..

He/She/It, + is + writing + a letter + now.

You/ We/ They + are + sleeping + now.

Assertive Negative

Form: **Subject +Am/Is/Are+NP + Ving + object + Time.**

e.g. : I + am + not + seeing + a film + now.

He/She/It, + is + not + writing + a letter + now.

You/ We/ They + are +not + sleeping + now.

Interrogative Positive

Form: **Present to be+ Subject + Ving + Object + Time + ?**

Am + I + seeing + a film + now +?

e.g. : Is + he/she/it + writing + a letter + now + ?

Are + you/ we/ they + sleeping + now + ?

Interrogative Negative

Form: **Present to be +Subject + NP + Ving + Object + Time + ?.**

Am + I + not + seeing + a film + now + ?

e.g. : Is + he/shc/it + not + writing + a letter + now + ?.

Are + you/ we/ they + not + sleeping + now + ?

SHORT FORMS

Note the following short forms of the modal verb with negative particle 'not'.

Assertive Negative

Form: **All Persons + am/is/are + NP + Ving + Object + T.**

I/He/They + ain't/isn"t/aren't + writing + a letter + now.

e.g. : I + ain 't + seeing + a film + now.

He/he/ It, + isn't + writing + a letter + now.

You/ We/ They +aren't +sleeping + now.

Interrogative Negative

Form: **Present to be + NP + Subject + Ving + Object + T +?**

Ain't/Isn't/Aren't + I/he/they + writing + a letter +now +?

e.g. Ain't + I + seeing + a film + now + ?

Isn't + he/she/it + writing + a letter + now + ?

Aren't + you/ we/ they + working + now + ?

PRESENT CONTINUOUS TENSE IS USED:

1. **to express an action which is in progress and is incomplete at the moment of speaking or writing. It is often associated with adverbs and adverbial phrases such as now, at present, at this moment etc. or when we want to talk about something that is happening at the time we are speaking, we use the Present Continuous. In order to emphasise the time of speaking, we often use adverbs and adverb phrases of present time like at the moment, just now, just, etc.**

   1. The baby is playing with the dog.
   2. *The boys are playing cricket.*
   3. *We are enjoying ice-creams.*
   4. *What are you doing now?*
   5. *My mother is making sweets at this moment.*
   6. *We are having a meeting. Come and join in.*
   7. *What is he doing? He is looking out of the window.*
   8. *I am feeling very tense just now.*

2.To express an action that will happen in the future. This is used to refer to activities planned for the future.

1. *They are going to Kashmir next summer.*
2. *She is coming to see us next week.*

to want, to wish, to desire, etc.

3. Certain miscellaneous verbs:

to posses, to own, to appear, to seem, to contain, to suit, to fit, to belong to, to matter, to consist of, etc.

These verbs, though not used in their collateral sense. Example:

1. *I am just seeing my friend off.*
2. *I am hearing lectures at the University.*
3. *Aunt Mary is minding the children.*
4. *He's always doubting my word.*
5. *What are you thinking of?*
6. *How are you liking your new job?*
7. *I think, you are being funny.*
8. *What's he wanting this time, I wonder.*

4. To express a future state or action with 'going to' as:

1. *When are you going to buy a new car?*
2. *We are going to visit them next month*
3. *The Chief Minister is flying to London tomorrow.*

NOTE: **Some verbs in English, on account of their meaning, do not normally occur in the continuous form.**

1. *The verb 'to be' when expressing a state.*
2. *Verbs of perception - to see, to hear, to smell, to taste, to feel.*

5A. Verbs which express knowledge, or belief, an opinion, supposition, a doubt, a hope, etc.

to know, to believe, to think, to suppose, to doubt, to hope etc

5B. Verbs of affection and disaffection:

to love, to adore, to like, to prefer, to mind, to object to, to dislike, to hate, to loathe, to abhor, to detest, etc.

Exercise 1

Fill in the blanks using the Simple Present or the Present Continuous Tense of the verbs given in bracket:

1. He ______ (go) to school now. He ______ (go) every day.

2. The coffee we _______ (drink) at present is very bitter.

3. Mother ______ (cook) some food in the kitchen at present; she always ______ (cook) there.

4. Our examination bell ______ (start) at 8 o'clock tomorrow.

5. The telephone bell ______ (ring) again. It sometimes ______ (ring) forty times a day.

6. I _____ (not tell) a lie in this case, and I always ______ (speak) the truth.

7. I shall tell him the news as soon as I ______ (see) him.

8. I ______ (do) my homework just now. I ______ (do) it every day.

9. She generally _______ (wear) a blue sari, but today she _____ (wear) a brown one.

10. She ______ (knit) now. She regularly ______ (knit) in the afternoon.

❑ ❑ ❑

Active Voice
Past Continuous Tense

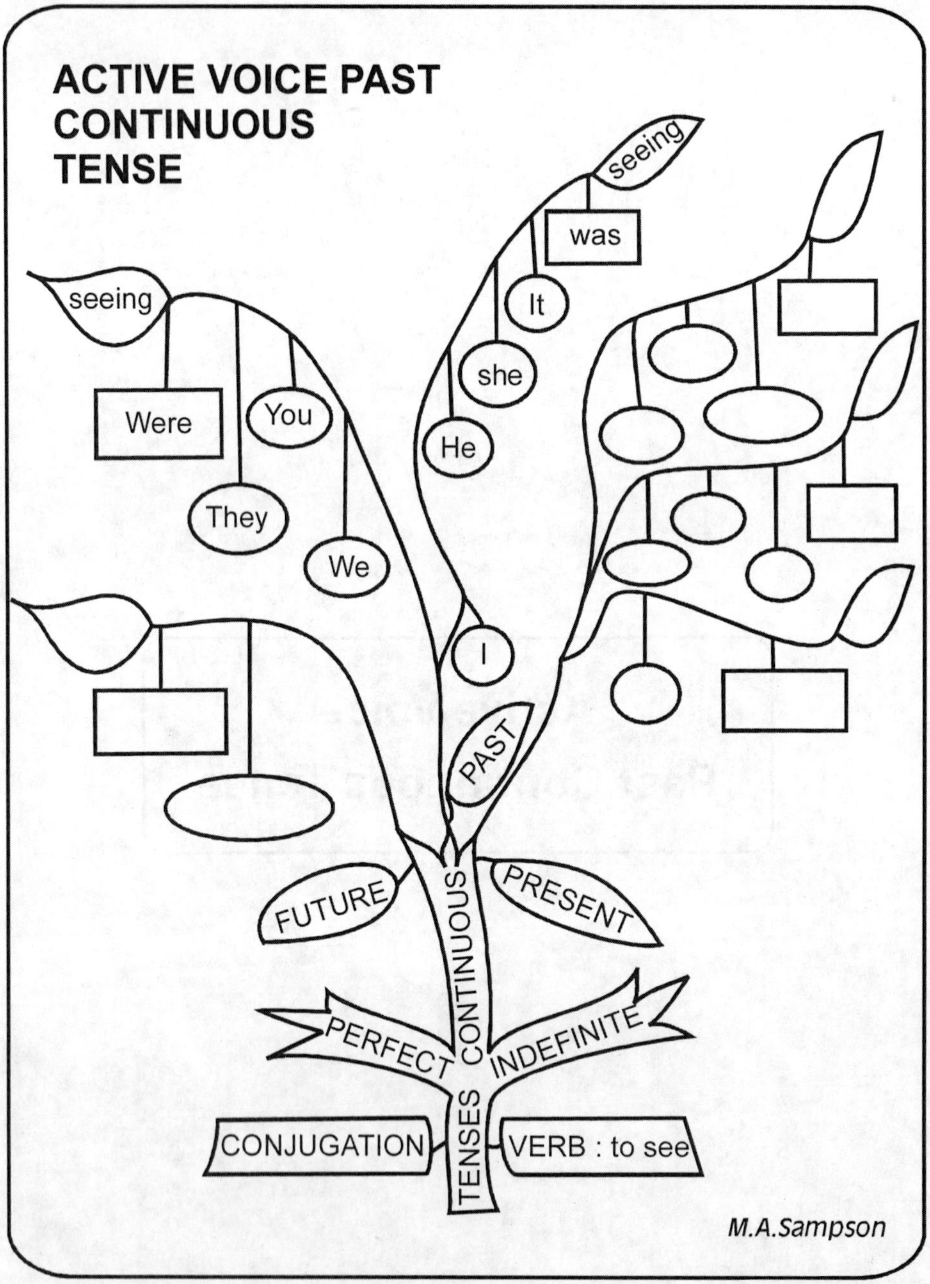

(Active Voice Continuous Tense Branch showing letters to Past Tense only)

Past Continuous Tense

Assertive Affirmative

Form: **S (All Persons) + Past to be + Ving + Object + Time.**
I + was + seeing + a film + yesterday at this time.

e.g. : I + was + seeing + a film +yesterday at this time.

He/he/ It +was + writing + a letter + when I saw him.

You/ We/ They + were + sleeping +yesterday at this time.

Assertive Negative

Form: **S (All Persons) + Past to be + NP + Ving + Object + Time.**
I + was + not + seeing + a film + yesterday at this time.

e.g. : I + was + not +seeing + a film + yesterday at this time.

He,She, It, + was + not + writing + a letter + when I saw him.

You, We, They + were + not + sleeping + yesterday at this time.

Interrogative Positive

Form: **Past tobe +Subject + Ving + Object + Time + ?**

Was + I + seeing + a film + yesterday at this time + ?

e.g. Was + I + seeing + a film + yesterday at this time + ?

Was + he,she,it + writing + a letter +yesterday at this time + ?

Were + you, we, they + sleeping + yesterday at this time + ?

Interrogative Negative

Form: **Past to be + Subject +NP + Ving + Object + T + ?**

Was/Were+he/they + not+writing + a letter + yesterday at this time + ?

e.g. Was + I + not + seeing + a film + yesterday at this time + ?

Was + he,she,it + not + writing + yesterday at this time + ?

Were + you/we/they + not + sleeping + yesterday at this time + ?

SHORT FORMS

Note the following short forms of the modal verb with negative particle 'not'.

Assertive Negative

Form: **All Persons + Past to be + NP + Ving + Object + Time.**

I/We + wasn't/weren't + writing + a letter + yesterday when I saw him.

e.g. : I + wasn 't + seeing + a film + yesterday at this time.

He,She, It, + wasn't + writing + a letter + when I saw him/her/it.

You, We, They + weren't + sleeping + yesterday at this time.

Interrogative Negative

Form: **Past to be + Subject + Ving + Object + T + ?**

wasn't/weren't + he/they + writing + a letter + yesterday at this time+?

e.g. Wasn't + I + seeing + a film + yesterday at this time + ?

Wasn't + he/she/it + writing + yesterday at this time + ?

Weren't + you/ we/ they + sleeping + yesterday at this time+?

THE PAST CONTINUOUS TENSE IS USED:

(1) To show that an action was commenced before and finished after a given moment or period of time in the past; as

(a) At four o'clock yesterday afternoon, I was playing chess.

(b) What was she doing where you called on her?

(c) When we arrived they were having lunch.

(d) It was raining when we reached the station.

(2) To express a continuous action associated with a period of time that is completely past or action in progress in the past:

(a) We were shopping all this morning.

(b) The children were playing all the afternoon.

(c) She was listening to the wireless all the evening.

(d) We were singing last night; so we could not come.

(e) It was raining all the afternoon.

(f) *I was working on my project last week*

(g) *She was writing letters all the morning.*

(3) To express two or more activities or states that were continuing at the same time; as

(a) *He was not listening while I was talking.*

(b) *While I was listening to the radio, Harry was painting a picture and Sheila was ironing the clothes.*

(4) To express intention with these verbs: going to, planning to, intending to; as,

(a) *I was going to inform you, but I forgot.*

(b) *She was planning to go to London, but she changed her mind.*

(c) *They were intending to buy a house when the prices rose.*

(5) With a time adverbial: When this tense is used with a time adverbial it suggests that the action probably began before that time and continued after that time; as,

(a) *At 9 o'clock, he was preparing the breakfast.*

(b) *At 10'clock, she was walking on the road.*

(6) To denote actions which began before something else happened: The Past Continuous and the Simple Past are often used together in a sentence. The Past Continuous describes a situation or action in progress in the past and the Simple Past describes a shorter action or event. The action or situation in progress is often introduced by Connectives like when, as, just as and while:

(a) *Just as I was leaving the school, I saw my mother.*

(b) *I recognised my friend when he was rushing to catch the train.*

(7) To indicate a more casual or less deliberate action: The Simple Past indicates a deliberate action; as,

(a) *I talked to the Head of the Department yesterday.*

(b) I was talking to the Head of the Department yesterday.

The first sentence suggests that the speaker had planned to that to the Head of the Department on some matter.

The second sentence suggests that the speaker had not planned to talk to him but happened to talk to him in a casual manner.

Exercise 1

Fill in the blanks using the Simple Present or the Present Continuous Tense of the verbs given in bracket:

1. He ______ (go) to school now. He ______ (go) every day.

2. The coffee we _______ (drink) at present is very bitter.

3. Mother ______ (cook) some food in the kitchen at present; she always ______ (cook) there.

4. Our examination bell ______ (start) at 8 o'clock tomorrow.

5. The telephone bell ______ (ring) again. It sometimes ______ (ring) forty times a day.

6. I ______ (not tell) a lie in this case, and I always ______ (speak) the truth.

7. I shall tell him the news as soon as I ______ (see) him.

8. I ______ (do) my homework just now. I ______ (do) it every day.

❒ ❒ ❒

Active Voice
Future Continuous Tense

ACTIVE VOICE FUTURE CONTINUOUS TENSE

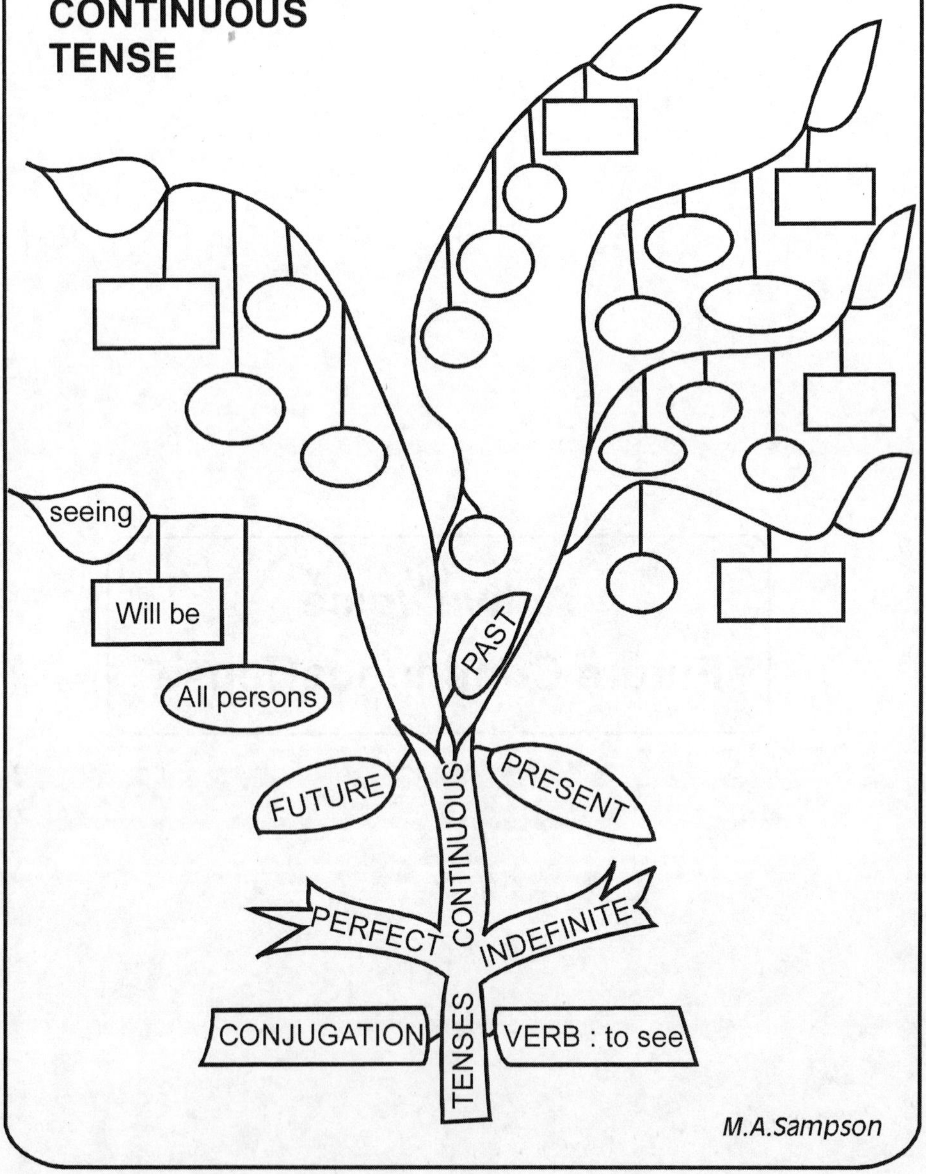

(Active Voice Continuous Tense Branch showing letters to Future Tense only)

Future Continuous Tense

Assertive Affirmative

Form: **First Person +shall + be + Ving + Object + Time**
I / We + shall + be + writing + a letter +tomorrow by this time.

e.g. You + will + be + writing + a letter + tomorrow by this time.

He + will + be + writing + a letter + tomorrow by this time.

She + will + be + singing + a song + tomorrow by this time.

They + will + be + digging + a hole + tomorrow by this time.

Assertive Negative

Form **Subject+M +NP + be + Ving + (Object) + Time.**

e.g. : I /We + shall +not +be + seeing + a film + tomorrow at this time.

He/She/It, + will + not + be + working + tomorrow at this time.

You/ They + will + not + be + working + tomorrow at this time.

Interrogative Positive

Form: **M + Subject + be + Ving + (Object)+ Time +?**

e.g. : Shall + I/we + be + seeing + a film + tomorrow at this time+?

Will + he/she/ it, + be + working + tomorrow at this time+?

Will + you/ we/ they + be + working + tomorrow at this time+?

Interrogative Negative

Form: Shall/Will+ S +NP + be + Ving +(Object) + Time.

e.g. : Shall + I + not + be + seeing + a film + tomorrow at this time?

Will + he/she/it+not + be+working + tomorrow at this time?

Will + you/we/they+not + be + working + tomorrow at this time?

SHORT FORMS

Note the following short forms of the modal verb with negative particle 'not'.

Assertive Negative

Form: **Subject+shall/will+NP+be+Ving +(Object) + Time.**

e.g. : I/We + shan't + be + seeing + a film + tomorrow at this time.
He/She/ It+won't + be + working + tomorrow at this time.
You/ They + won't + be + working + tomorrow at this time.

Interrogative Negative

Form:

M+NP+ S + be + Ving + (Object) + Time?

e.g.: Shan't+I + be + seeing + a film + tomorrow at this time?
Won't+ he/she/ it+be + working + tomorrow at this time?
Won't+ you/ we/ they + be + working+ tomorrow at this time?

THE FUTURE CONTINUOUS IS USED:

1. to express an action which will occur in the usual course of events.

e.g. *(1) She will be staying here till Sunday.*
(2) I will be meeting him tomorrow.
(3) The children will be playing here this evening.

2. to express future without intention:

e.g. *(1) He won't be staying long.*
(2) The lady will be coming back this way.
(3) Will you be going to England?

3. to predict what we think will happen; as,

(1) The festival will last *for a week.*
(2) One day people will travel *to Mars.*
(3) We will win *the match.*

4. to indicate an offer or a promise; as

(1) I shall post *that letter for you.*
(2) I will give *you a gift, if you* pass.

5. to indicate an instant decision (at the moment of speaking); **as**

(1) It is *very hot. I* will put *on the fan.*
(2) It is *my birthday. We* will have *a party.*

(6) after verbs and verb phrases like be sure, think, expect, suppose, hope, believe, etc; as,

(a) I hope he will come *tomorrow.*

(b) I'm sure it will be *all right.*

(c) I expect *we* will win *the match.*

Exercise

Fill in the blanks with the **Future Continuous form** of the verbs given in the brackets:

1. At this time tomorrow I ______ (enjoy) myself in Mussorie.

2. She ______ (wait) outside her office for you this evening.

3. At his time next month you ______ (travel) in Australia.

4. It probably ______ (rain) when your mother gets back from her office.

5. They _____ (reach) Bhutan on Sunday.

6. If you go there now, they _____ (have) dinner.

7. When you come tomorrow morning, I ______ (have) my dance.

8. If you come before noon, I _____ (wait) for you in my cabin.

9. They ______ (spend) the winter in Kullu.

10. If you svisit her on Sunday morning, she probably _____ (practise) the piano.

❑ ❑ ❑

SHORT FORMS

to be:	am, is , are, was, were
M:	Modal Verbs like will should etc.
NP:	Negative Particle 'no' and 'not'
S:	Subject or Subject Phrase
O:	Object or Object Phrase
V:	Present Tense form of the verb like go, write etc.
Vs:	Present tense form 's' added to it belonging to third person, singular number and present tense e.g. writes, does, goes, is, has etc.
Ving:	Present Participle form of the verb like writing, coming, bringing etc.
Ven:	Past participle form of the verb like written, sung, brought, pulled etc.
T:	Time Phrase
All Persons:	I,we,;you;he,she,It,they

Active Voice

Perfect Tense Branch

- Present
- Past
- Future

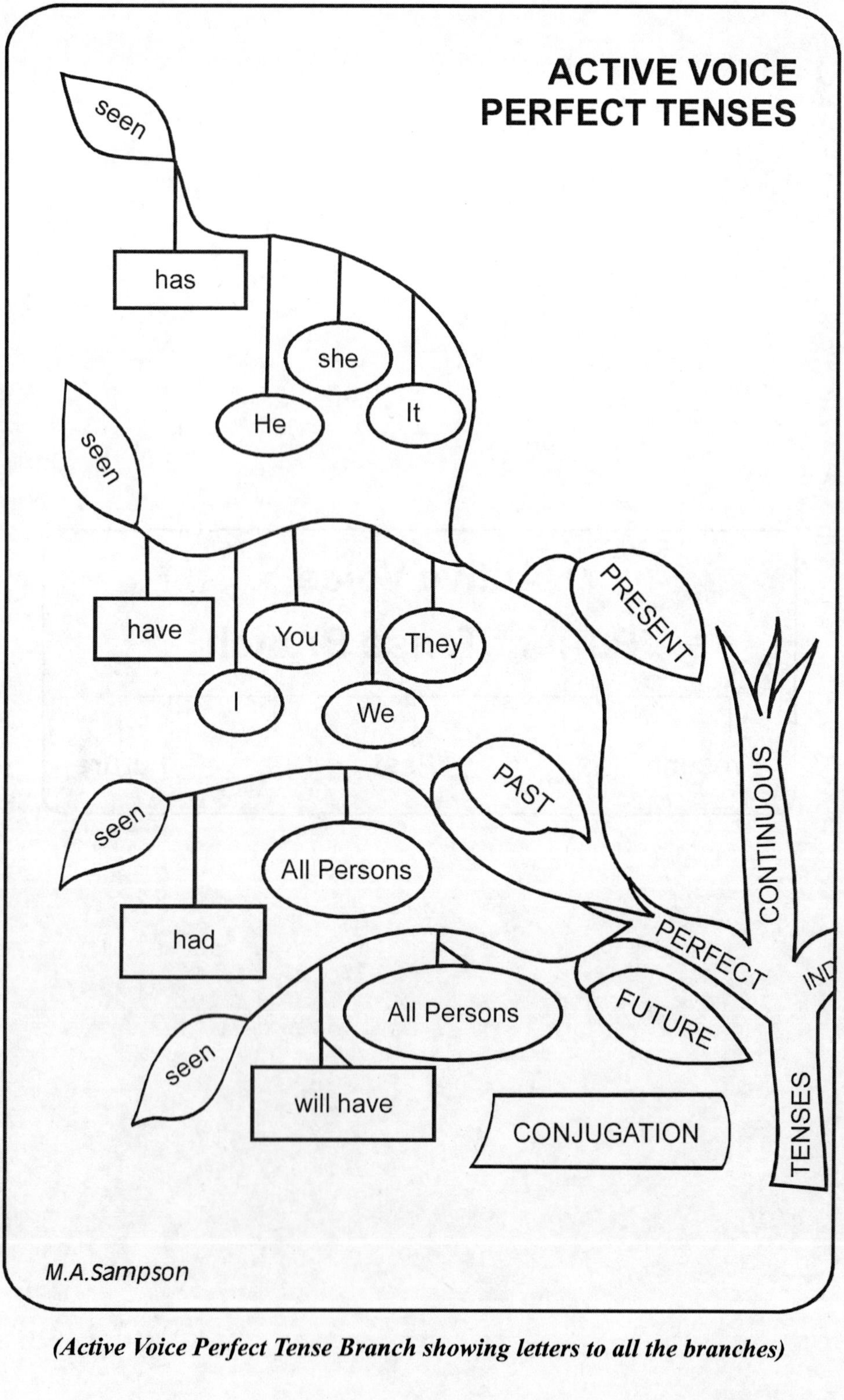

(Active Voice Perfect Tense Branch showing letters to all the branches)

PERFECT TENSE BRANCH

Present **Past** **Future**

PRESENT PERFECT TENSE: The sentences which state that the work has been completed but it was completed recently.

e.g. I have written two letters just now.

PAST PERFECT TENSE: Those sentences by which we come to know that in the past the work was fully completed.

e.g. I had gone home before you came to my office.

FUTURE PERFECT TENSE: The sentences which state that work is going to be fully completed by given future point of time.

e.g. My clerk will have finished the given work before I come to office tomorrow.

SHORT FORMS

to be:	am, is , are, was, were
M:	Modal Verbs like will should etc.
NP:	Negative Particle 'no' and 'not'
S:	Subject or Subject Phrase
O:	Object or Object Phrase
V:	Present Tense form of the verb like go, write etc.
Vs:	Present tense form 's' added to it belonging to third person, singular number and present tense e.g. writes, does, goes, is, has etc.
Ving:	Present Participle form of the verb like writing, coming, bringing etc.
Ven:	Past participle form of the verb like written, sung, brought, pulled etc.
T:	Time Phrase
All Persons:	I,we,;you;he,she,It,they

Active Voice
Present Perfect Tense

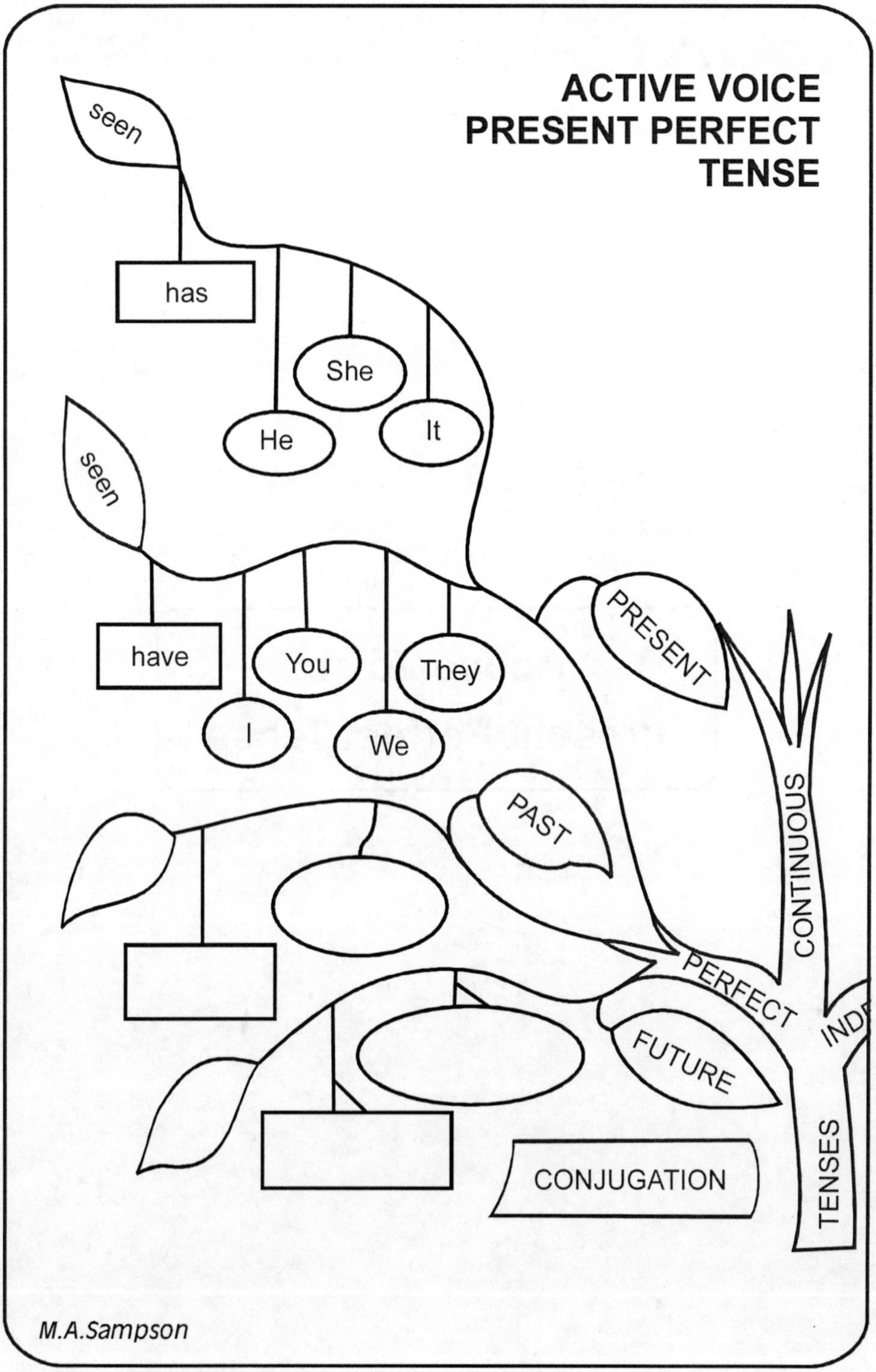

(Active Voice Perfect Tense Branch showing letters to Present Tense only)

Present Perfect Tense

Assertive Affirmative

Form: **Subject + have/has + Ven + Object + Time.**

e.g. I//We/You/They + have + drawn + a picture + just now.

He/She + has + written + a letter +j ust now.

It + has + fallen + just in the morning.

Assertive Negative

Form: **Subject + have/has +NP + Ven + Object + Time.**

e.g. I//We/You/They + have +not + drawn + a picture + just now.

He/She + has + not + written + a letter + just now.

It + has + not + fallen + just in the morning.

Interrogative Positive

Form: **Have/Has + Subject + Ven + Object + Time +?**

e.g. Have + I//we/you/they + drawn + a picture + just now + ?

Has + he/she + written + a letter + just now + ?

Has + it + fallen + just in the morning + ?

Interrogative Negative

Form: **Have/Has +Subject +NP +Ven + Object + Time?**

e.g. Have + I//we/you/they + not + drawn + a picture + just now?

Has + he/she + not + written + a letter +just now?

Has + it +not + fallen +just in the morning?

SHORT FORMS

Note the following short forms of the modal verb with negative particle 'not'.

Assertive Negative

Form: **Subject + M +NP+ Ven +(Object)+ Time.**

e.g. I//We/You/They + haven't+ drawn +a picture + just now.

He/She + hasn't + written +a letter +just now.

It + hasn't + fallen + just in the morning.

Interrogative Negative

Form: **M+NP + Subject +Ven +(Object) +Time?**

e.g. Haven't + I//we/you/they +drawn +a picture+just now?

Hasn't + he/she + written +a letter + just now?

Hasn't + it + fallen + just in the morning?

PRESENT PERFECT TENSE IS USED FOR :

Denoting action that has just been completed, as:

Have you finished your lesson, Harry?

I have not finished yet, Father.

I have already finished, Father.

I have just finished, Father.

(1) As is shown by the name, the Present Perfect is used when we are thinking more about the present than about the past. For this reason, this tense is often associated with adverbs or adverbial phrases of present time, such as now, today, recently, this week (month, year, etc.), several; as

(a) She has finished her breakfast now.

(b) She has *not* come *here today.*

(c) He has *recently* bought *a new car.*

(d) We have told *her several times not to be rude to her mother.*

(e) All my working life I have waited *for a better future.*

(f) I have *always* felt *that films should be entertaining.*

(g) *I* have finished *writing ten pages so far today.*

(h) *I* have *never* seen *an octopus before.*

2. The Present Perfect Tense is often used with "ever", in questions; as:

(a) *Have you ever been up in a balloon?*

(b) *Have you ever been to London? (i.e. at any time up to the present)*

3. It also denotes a completed action or occurence which is connected through its result with the present moment; as

(a) *He* has purchased *a new car.*

(b) *My father* has seen *the Taj Mahal.*

(c) *He* has been *a teacher, a journalist, a sales representative, and now he is a minister.*

(d) *It* has rained *heavily during the night.*

(e) *The sun* has set.

(f) *We* have *just* finished *our tea.*

4. It is also used with before, when before means *'sometime in the past, reckoning back from the present moment'.*

(a) *I'*ve seen *that film before.*

(b) *I'*ve seen *her somewhere before.*

5. It is sometimes used to express an experience which the speaker or the writer has had; as

(a) *I* have seen *many a young man ruined by drink.*

(b) *I* have seen *people die of starvation.*

6. It is used to indicate the future in a subordinate clause; as

(a) *I* shall write *a letter when I* have finished *my dinner.*

(b) *I* shall play *tennis after I* have finished *my homework.*

7. It is used to indicate habit with when, before, after, etc.

(A) Do *you ever* go *to bed before you* have finished *your work?*

No, I never go *to bed before I* have finished *my work.*

Yes, I sometimes go *to bed before I* have finished *my work.*

❐ ❐ ❐

SHORT FORMS

to be:	am, is , are, was, were
M:	Modal Verbs like will should etc.
NP:	Negative Particle 'no' and 'not'
S:	Subject or Subject Phrase
O:	Object or Object Phrase
V:	Present Tense form of the verb like go, write etc.
Vs:	Present tense form 's' added to it belonging to third person, singular number and present tense e.g. writes, does, goes, is, has etc.
Ving:	Present Participle form of the verb like writing, coming, bringing etc.
Ven:	Past participle form of the verb like written, sung, brought, pulled etc.
T:	Time Phrase
All Persons:	I,we,;you;he,she,It,they

Active Voice
Past Perfect Tense

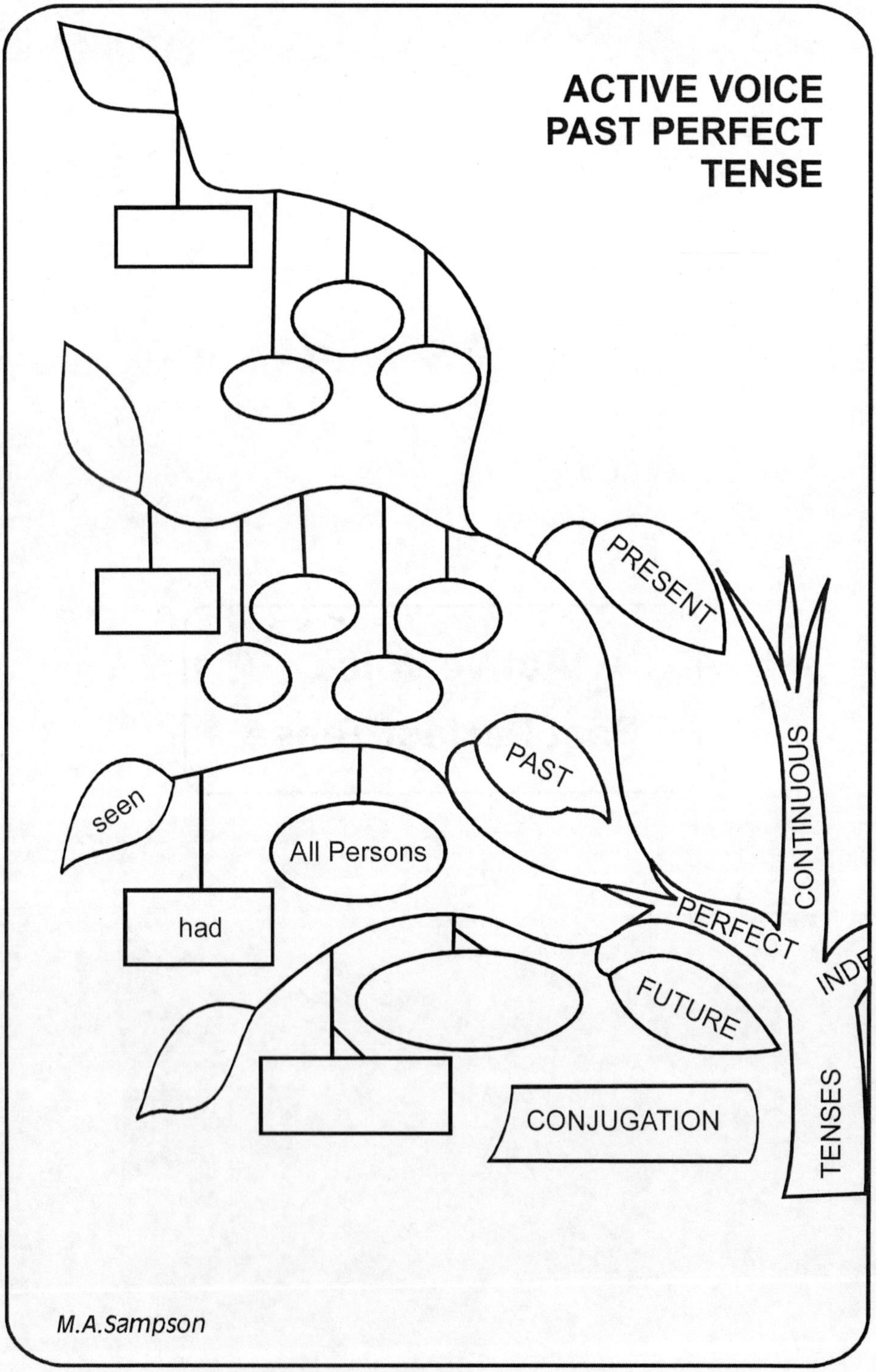

(Active Voice Perfect Tense Branch showing letters to Past Tense only)

Past Perfect Tense

Assertive Affirmative

***Form*: All Persons + had + Ven + Object + Time.**

e.g. I//We/You/They + had + drawn + a picture + just now.

He/She + had + written + a letter + just now.

It + had + fallen + just in the morning.

Assertive Negative

***Form:* All Persons + had+NP + Ven + Object + Time.**

e.g. I//We/You/They + had +not + drawn + a picture + before you came.

He/She +had+not + written + a letter+before you saw them.

It + had+not + fallen + in the morning.

Interrogative Positive

***Form:* Had +All Persons + Ven +Object + Time +?**

e.g. Had + I//we/you/they +drawn + a picture + before you came+?

Had + he/she + written + a letter + before you saw them+?

Had + it + fallen + in the morning + ?

Interrogative Negative

***Form:* Had +All Persons + not + Ven +Object + Time?**

e.g. Had + I//we/you/they + not+drawn +a picture+ before you came?

Had + he/she + not+written+a letter+before you saw them?

Had + it + not + fallen + in the morning?

SHORT FORMS

Note the following short forms of the modal verb with negative particle 'not'.

Assertive Negative

Form: **Subject + had+NP + Ven + Object + Time.**

e.g. I//We/You/They+ hadn't + drawn+ a picture+ before you came.

He/She + hadn't + written + a letter + before you saw them.

It + hadn't + fallen + in the morning.

Interrogative Negative

Form: **Had+NP+ Subject + Ven + Object + Time +?**

e.g. Hadn't + I//we/you/they +drawn + a picture + before you came+?

Hadn't + he/she + written + a letter + before you saw them+?

Hadn't + it + fallen + in the morning+?

THE PAST PERFECT TENSE IS USED:

to show an action completed before a certain moment in the past.

e.g. *I met my friend in Mumbai in 1880. I had seen him last, five years before.*

(A) If two actions are concerned in the past, the earlier action is to be in the Past Perfect and the other in the Simple Past.

e.g. *(1) After she had taken her lunch, she went to the theatre.*

(2) The fire had burnt the house down by the time the fire force arrived.

(3) When I reached the station, the train had departed.

(B) The Past Perfect is never used with adverbs of Past time; but Simple past is used.

e.g. *(1) I had met him yesterday. (wrong)*

I met him yesterday. (correct)

(2) *She had come here last day. (Wrong)*

She came here last day. (Right)

1. Reference to an earlier past ,

The Past Perfect tense shows an action completed before a certain moment in the past.

When from a certain point in the past, a person looks back on an earlier action we use the past perfect; as,

(a) *I* met *my friend in Mumbai in 1880. I* had seen *him last, five years before.*

(b) *I* met *my friend in 1995. I* had *already* met *his father five years earlier.*

(c) *The whole complex* was *in chaos. The police* had demolished *all the floors of the building.*

2. To distinguish between two actions in the past:

When we want to emphasize that the two actions did not take place simultaniously, i.e., the first action was completed before the second one started, we use the past perfect tense; as

If two actions are concerned in the past, the earlier action is to be in the Past Perfect and the other in the Simple Past.

(a) *After she* had taken *her lunch, she went to the theatre.*

(b) *The fire* had burnt *the house down by the time the fire force arrived.*

(c) *When I* reached *the station, the train* had departed.

(d) *The patient* had died *when the doctor arrived.* (i.e. the patient was already dead when the doctor arrived)

(e) *She* had lost *her job as a manger and was working as a waitress.* (She lost job first and then began to work as a waitress)

Some adverbs *(e.g. already, ever, for just, never*, etc.) are often used ithe the past perfect to emphasize the sequence of events; as

(a) When he entered the classroom the teacher *had already* left.

(b) We *had just finished* the work when the Chief Guest arrived.

3. In conditional clauses; as

(a) *If I* had known *you were ill, I would have come to see you.*

(b) Had I known *the doctor was around, I should have discussed my problem with him.*

❐ ❐ ❐

SHORT FORMS

to be:	am, is , are, was, were
M:	Modal Verbs like will should etc.
NP:	Negative Particle 'no' and 'not'
S:	Subject or Subject Phrase
O:	Object or Object Phrase
V:	Present Tense form of the verb like go, write etc.
Vs:	Present tense form 's' added to it belonging to third person, singular number and present tense e.g. writes, does, goes, is,has etc.
Ving:	Present Participle form of the verb like writing, coming, bringing etc.
Ved:	Past Tense form of the verb like wrote, sang, pulled, brought etc.
Ven:	Past participle form of the verb like written, sung, brought, pulled etc.
T:	Time Phrase
All Persons:	I,we,;you;he,she,It,they

Active Voice

Future Perfect Tense

(Active Voice Perfect Tense Branch showing letters to Future Tense only)

Future Perfect Tense

Assertive Affirmative

Form: **First Person + shall + have + Ven + Object + Time.**

I/We + shall + have + written + a letter + by this time tomorrow.

Form: **Second/Third Persons + will + have +Ven +Object + Time.**

You/They/ He/She/It + willl +have + written+a letter +by this time.

e.g. He + will + have + written + a letter + by this time tomorrow.

She + will + have + sung + a song + by this time tomorrow.

They + will + have + dug + a hole + by this time tomorrow.

Assertive Negative

Form: **First Person + shall + NP + have +Ven + Object + Time.**

I/We +shall+ not +have+written+a letter.+by this time tomorrow.

Form: **Second/Third Persons + will+NP +have+ Ven + O +T.**

You/They/He/She/It +willl+not+have+ written+a letter+by this time tomorrow.

e.g. He + will + have + written + a letter + by this time tomorrow.

She + will + have + sung + a song + by this time tomorrow.

They + will + have + dug + a hole + by this time tomorrow.

Interrogative Positive

Form: **M + First Person + Have + Ven + Object + Time + ?**

Shall + I/we + have + written + a letter + by this time tomorrow +?

Form: **M + Second/Third Persons + have + Ven +Object + T+?**

Will + you/they/he/she/it + have + written + a letter + by this time tomorrow + ?

e.g. Shall +I/we + have + written + a letter.+by this time tomorrow+?

Will +he/ she /they + have + sung + a song + by this time tomorrow+?

Interrogative Negative

Form: **M + First Person + Have + NP +Ven + Object +Time + ?**

Shall + I/we+have+not+written+a letter+by this time tomorrow +?

Form: **M+ Second/Third Persons +have+not +Ven +Object +Time+?**

Will + you/they/he/she/it + have + not + written + a letter + by this time tomorrow + ?

e.g. Shall +I/we+ have + not + written + a letter.+ by this time tomorrow+?

Will +he/ she /they + have + not + sung + a song +by this time tomorrow + ?

SHORT FORMS

Note the following short forms of the modal verb with negative particle 'not'.

Assertive Negative

Form: **Subject + shan't + have + Ven + Object +Time.**

I//We +shan't + have + drawn + a picture + by this time tomorrow.

Form: **Subject + won't + have + Ven + Object + Time.**

You/They /He/She + won't + have+ drawn + a picture + by this time tomorrow.

It + won't + have + fallen + by this time tomorrow.

Interrogative Negative

Form: **M + NP + First Person + Have + Ven + Object + Time**

Shan't + I/we + have + written +a letter + by this time tomorrow +?

Form: **M+NP+Second/ Third Persons + have+Ven+Object + Time+?**

Won't + you/they/he/she/it + have + written + a letter + by this time tomorrow+?

e.g. Shan't +I/we + have + written + a letter.+ by this time tomorrow+?

Won't+he/she/they +have +sung + a song + by this time tomorrow+?

❐ ❐ ❐

EXERCISE

Choose the correct verb form from those in brackets:

1. The earth _____ round the sun. (move, moves, moved)
2. My friends _______ the Prime Minister yesterday. (see, have seen, saw)
3. I _____ him only one letter up to now. (sent, have sent, shall send)
4. I shall telephone you when he ____ back. (comes, will come, came)
5. It started to rain while we _____ tennis. (are playing, were playing, had played)
6. Can I have some milk before I ____ to bed? (go, am going, shall go)
7. He _____ asleep while he was driving. (falls, fell, has fallen)
8. I'm sure I _____ him at the party last night. (saw, have seen, had seen)
9. He ____ a mill in this town. (have, has, is having)
10. He ____ here for the last five years. (worked, is working, has been working)

❐ ❐ ❐

SHORT FORMS

to be: am, is , are, was, were

M: Modal Verbs like will should etc.

NP: Negative Particle 'no' and 'not'

S: Subject or Subject Phrase

O: Object or Object Phrase

V: Present Tense form of the verb like go, write etc.

Vs: Present tense form 's' added to it belonging to third person, singular number and present tense e.g. writes, does, goes, is,has etc.

Ving: Present Participle form of the verb like writing, coming, bringing etc.

Ved: Past Tense form of the verb like wrote, sang, pulled, brought etc.

Ven: Past participle form of the verb like written, sung, brought, pulled etc.

T: Time Phrase

All Persons: I,we,;you;he,she,It,they

Section - 2
Passive Voice

SHORT FORMS

to be:	am, is , are, was, were
M:	Modal Verbs like will should etc.
NP:	Negative Particle 'no' and 'not'
S:	Subject or Subject Phrase
O:	Object or Object Phrase
V:	Present Tense form of the verb like go, write etc.
Vs:	Present tense form 's' added to it belonging to third person, singular number and present tense e.g. writes, does, goes, is,has etc.
Ving:	Present Participle form of the verb like writing, coming, bringing etc.
Ved:	Past Tense form of the verb like wrote, sang, pulled, brought etc.
Ven:	Past participle form of the verb like written, sung, brought, pulled etc.
T:	Time Phrase
All Persons:	I,we,;you;he,she,It,they

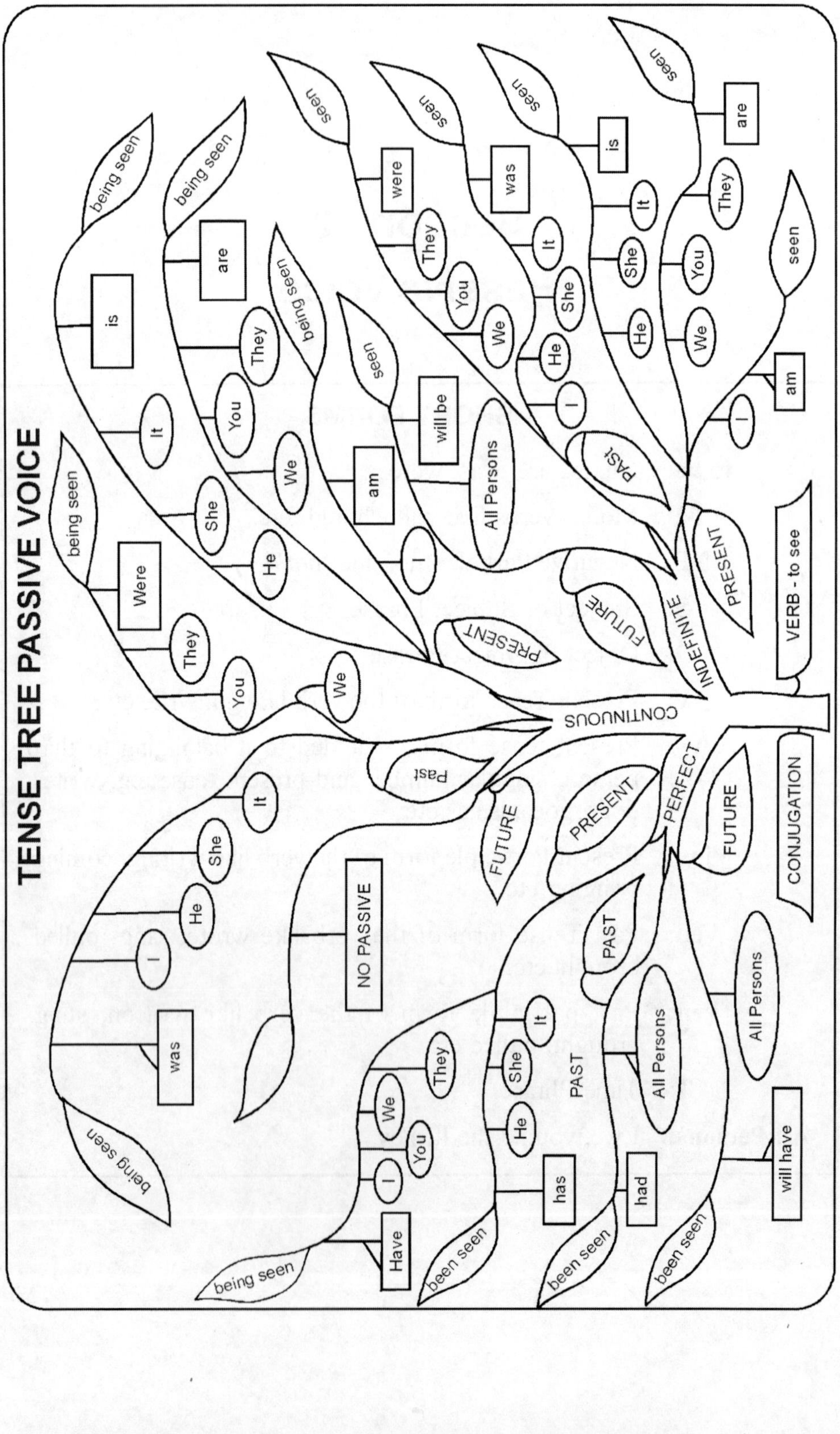
TENSE TREE PASSIVE VOICE
VERB - to see
CONJUGATION
INDEFINITE
CONTINUOUS
PERFECT
PRESENT
PAST
FUTURE
I
am
seen
He
She
It
is
We
You
They
are
was
were
All Persons
will be
being seen
Were
Past
NO PASSIVE
Have
has
had
will have
been seen

Passive Voice

Depending on the time sense the Active Voice and Passive Voices are divided into three different main branches namely Indefinite tenses, Continuous tenses, and Perfect Tenses.

The Second Section of the book deals with the Passive Voice Tenses. ***A verb is in the Passive Voice when its form shows that something is done to the person or thing denoted by the subject.***

The branches **Indefinite, Continuous** and **Perfect** are further divided into three small branches depending on whether the action stated in the verb of the sentence does not pin point the exact time when it takes place (Indefiniteness): whether the action is still continuing at the given point of time in ***present*** time, past time or in the ***future*** time and whether the action is completed fully at the given point may it be in the *present* time, *past* time or in the *future* time.

The figure of the Passive Voice Tense tree gives,at glance, the ***scope of tenses*** it has in it. As in the Active Voice tree each branch has seven personal pronouns attached to it and the pronouns are grouped under the appropriate verb that they take. The verb form is given on the leaf of the branch at the end. If the verb has any additional verbs like modal and helping verbs they are given on the **placards** (board) hung to the branch at the appropriate place.

Rationale

Reasons for learning and mastering English Voices can be summed up in ***Five*** good reasons.

1. In vernacular languages more than 90% of sentences are of Active Voices. For instances we do not say, The mango was eaten by me' in our vernacular language. If you try to say it sounds funny. Hence, while teaching vernacular grammar the passive voice teaching is almost neglected or at least undertoned. In English language, however, it is all right to say, ' The mango was eaten by me.' Active and passive voice sentences in English language are almost fifty percent of each type. Hence **it becomes imperative** to learn voices in English language.

2. Some times the writer wants to omit the doer of the action deliberately. In that case he has to write the passive voice sentence. We cannot omit the doer if the sentence is active. Therefore he should know how to convert active voice sentence into passive voice. e.g. Shah Jahan built Taj Mahal. We can omit Shah Jahan (the doer) by writing this sentence as The Taj Mahal was built in 1763.(still the sentence is good enough to be called as complete sentence.)

3. Active Voice sentence changed into passive voice sentence both do not mean exactly the same. Though their grammatical meaning is the same, shade in the meaning differs. Passive voice sentence acquires legal tone along with the usually transposition of the words and change in the finite verb form. e.g. When a Principal of the college sends a notice saying 'I want to take a meeting' rather than,'A meeting is to be held today at 9 a.m. second type has a tone of compulsion and the first one is suggests if you can attend. Hence notices with passive voice sentences give a sense of authority.

4. As a corollary to above when a complaint letter or a letter for collection of dues active voice paragraph may be too informal for complying with the request of collection or redressal for the damage of goods for which the complaint letter is to be written. It is effective if greeting part of the paragraph to be written in active voice sentences and complaint part in the passive voice sentences as, invariably you would like to omit the doer who caused the damage to the consignment you were supposed to get safely.Hence the need to specialize in this competency.

5. It is interesting to note that all the legal ***Acts*** of criminal or civil codes are written in passive voice. Even the judgment passed by the court is in passive voice. ***Therefore it becomes imperative*** for all the citizens to acquire the ability to understand to write correctly and efficiently the passive voice sentences. ***This book is meant to lead you towards the accuracy in this ability.***

_____Author

Passive Voice Indefinite Tenses

PASSIVE VOICE INDEFINITE TENSES

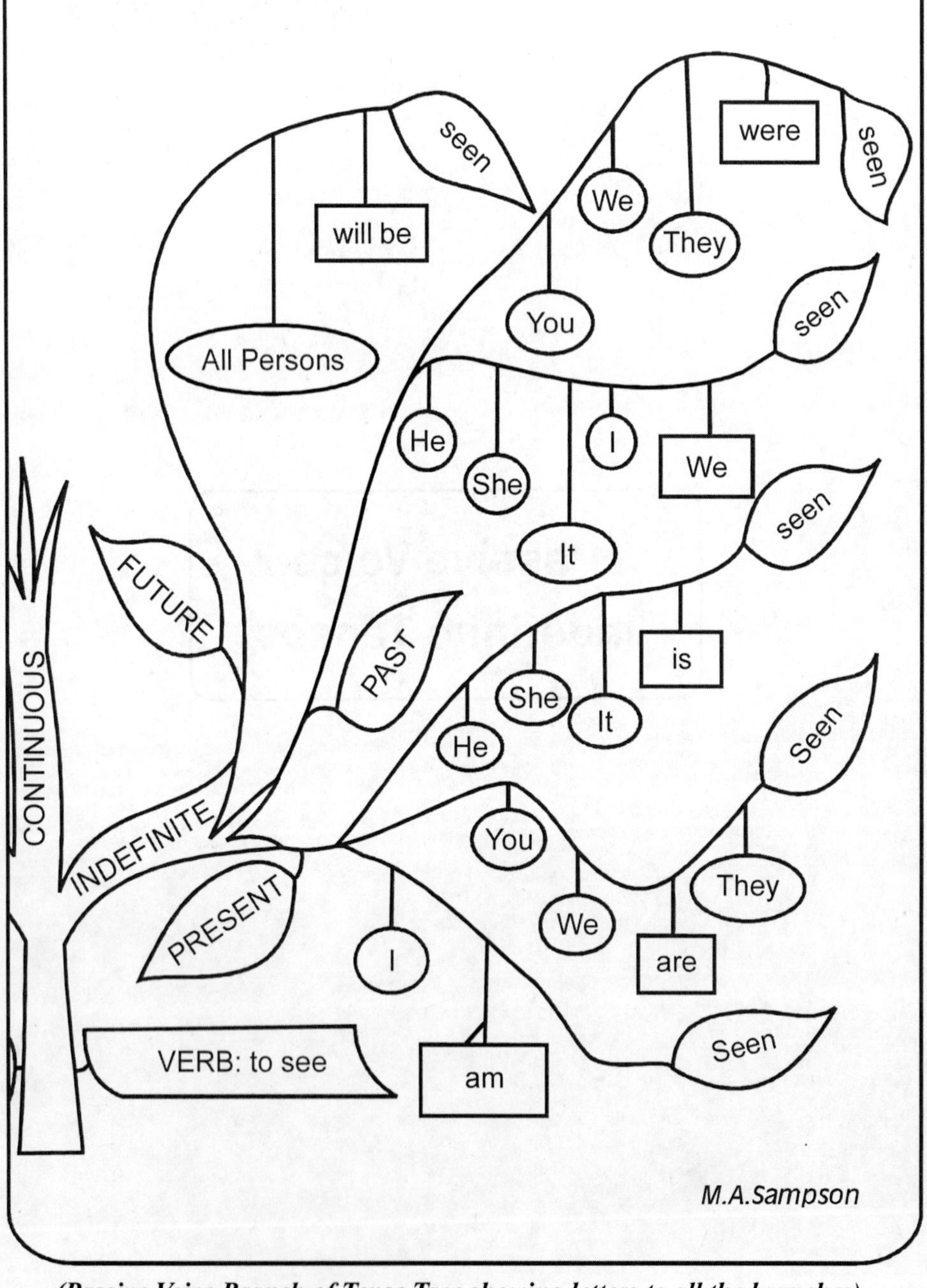

(Passive Voice Branch of Tense Tree showing letters to all the branches)

Passive Voice

Indefinite Tense Branch

Present **Past** **Future**

This branch of the tense deals with the indefiniteness of the time in present, ast and future. It describes the action which has taken place in the present, past or future but does not pin point the time at which it has taken place. Therefore sentences of this type come under the tense known as Indefinite tense.

1. Present Tense:

An award is given by the President

A song is sung by each student.

2. Past Tense:

Last mont an award was given away by the president.

The songs were sung by the girls in their turn.

3. Future Tense:

An award will be given by the Principal at the function next week.

After the function the National Anthem will be sung by a special group.

❑ ❑ ❑

SHORT FORMS

to be: am, is , are, was, were

M: Modal Verbs like will should etc.

NP: Negative Particle 'no' and 'not'

S: Subject or Subject Phrase

O: Object or Object Phrase

V: Present Tense form of the verb like go, write etc.

Vs: Present tense form 's' added to it belonging to third person, singular number and present tense e.g. writes, does, goes, is,has etc.

Ving: Present Participle form of the verb like writing, coming, bringing etc.

Ved: Past Tense form of the verb like wrote, sang, pulled, brought etc.

Ven: Past participle form of the verb like written, sung, brought, pulled etc.

T: Time Phrase

All Persons: I,we,;you;he,she,It,they

Passive Voice
Indefinite Present Tense

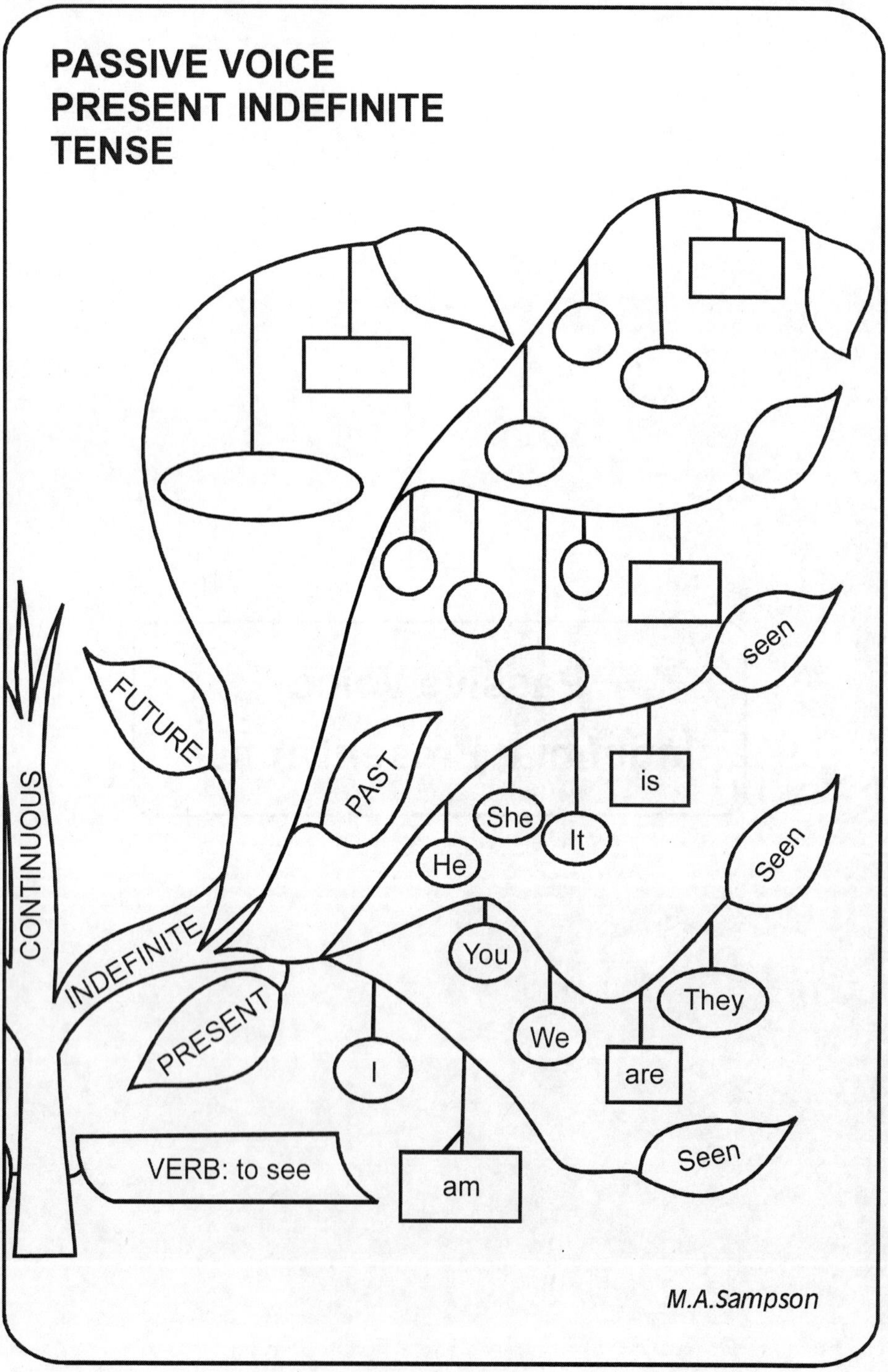

(Passive Voice Indefinite Tense showing Present Tense branch only)

Present Indefinite Tense

(The Simple Present)

Assertive Affirmative

Form: **Subject + to be + Ven + by + Agent + T.**

I + am + seen + by + them + everyday.

You + are + seen + by + them + everyday.

He/She/It + is + seen + by + them + everyday.

They + are + seen + by + him + everyday.

In the Present Simple (Indefinite Tense), the verb shows that the event was completed at a point of time in the present but does not specify exact time when the event took place.***We must have a part of the sentence to show that the event has taken place in the present*** In the model example 'everyday'does that work. If, however, this part is not given in the sentence of this tense the time '**present time**' is understood.

a. A letter is written by her everyday.

b. Letters are written by them regularly.

From the Indefinite branch, it can be seen that there are three auxiliaries, '**am**'*,for the pronoun 'I',* '**is**'*for pronouns, 'He', She'snd 'It'; and* '**are**'*for pronouns 'You', 'We', and ' They' as shown on the three placards attached to three different branches-compare the figure at the left.*

All the rest of the attributes of this tense are as described for Active present indefinite tense.

Assertive Negative

Form: **S + to be + NP + Ven + by + Agent + T**

I + am + not + seen + by + them + everyday.

You + are + not + seen + by + them + everyday.

He/She/It + is + not + seen + by + them + everyday.

They + are + not + seen + by + him + everyday.

Interrogative Positive

Form: To be+Subject + Ven + by +Agent + T + ?

Am + I + seen + by +them + everyday + ?

Are + you + seen + by +them +everyday + ?.

Is + he/she/it + seen + by +them + everyday + ?

Are + they + seen + by + him + everyday + ?

Interrogative Negative

Form: To be+ S + NP +Ven + by + Agent + T + ?

Am + I + not + seen + by + them + everyday + ?

Are + you + not + seen + by + them + everyday + ?

Is + he/she/it + not + seen + by + them + everyday + ?

Are + they + not + seen + by + him +everyday +?

SHORT FORMS

Note the following short forms of the modal verb with negative particle 'not'.

Assertive Negative

Form: **Subject + to be+NP + Ven + by + Agent + T.**

I + ain't + seen + by + them + everyday.

You + aren't + seen + by + them + everyday.

He/She/It + isn't + seen + by + them + everyday.

They + aren't + seen + by + him + everyday.

Interrogative Negative

Form: **To be+NP + Subject + Ven + by + Agent + T + ?**

Ain't + I + seen + by + them + everyday + ?

Aren't + you + seen + by + them + everyday + ?.

Isn't + he/she/it + seen + by + them + everyday + ?

Aren't + they + seen + by + him + everyday + ?

❐ ❐ ❐

Passive Voice
Indefinite Past Tense

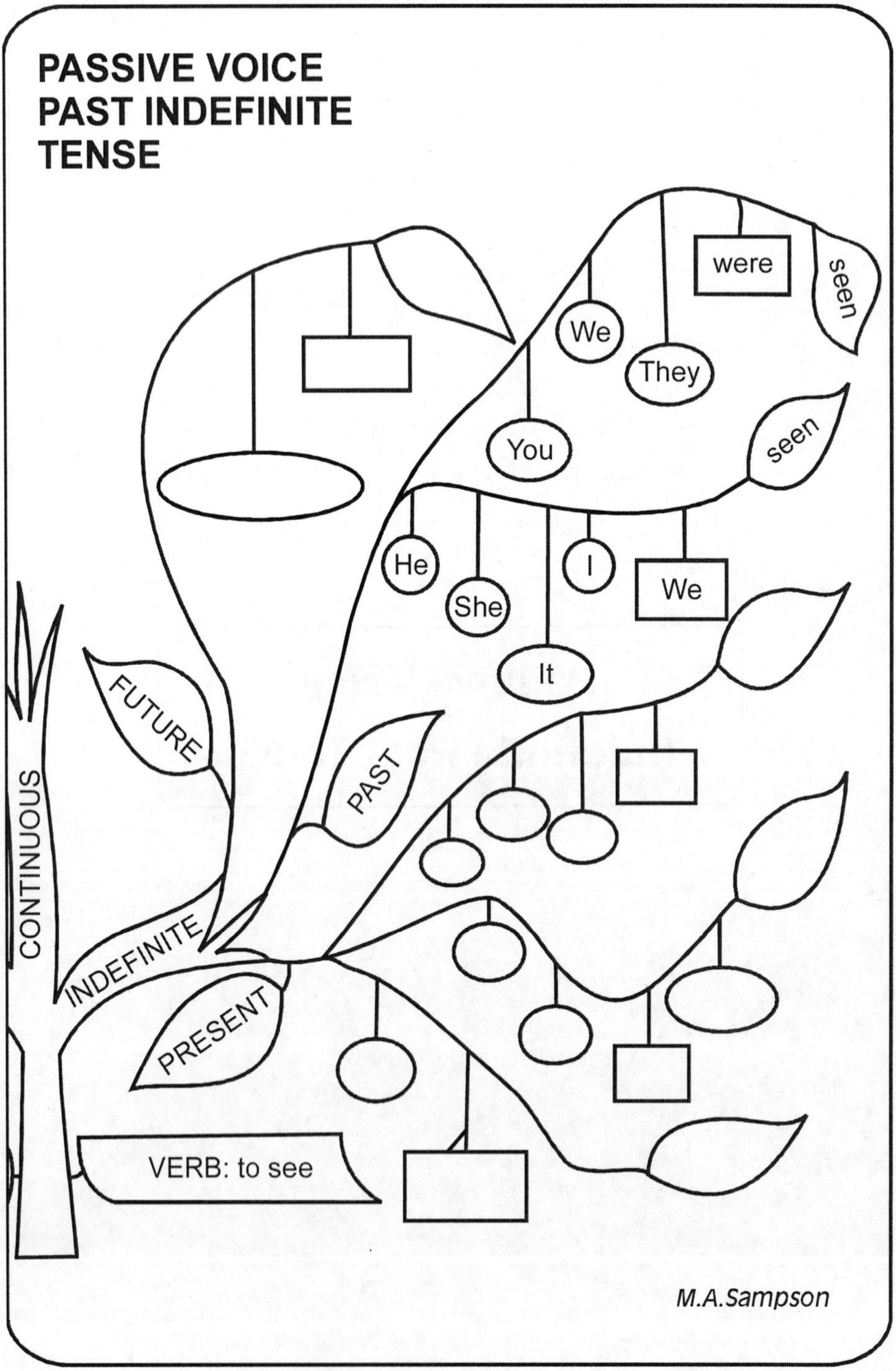

(Passive Voice Indefinite Tense showing Past Tense branch only)

Past Indefinite Tense

Assertive Affirmative

Form: **Subject + to be + Ven + by + Agent + T.**

I + was + seen + by + them + before.

They + were + seen + by + her + before.

In the Past Simple (Indefinite Tense), the verb shows that the event was completed at a point of time in the past and thus it is separated from the present.

a. A letter was written by her yesterday.

b. Letters were written by them two days before.

From the above sentence, it can be seen that there are two auxiliaries, **'was'** *for pronoun 'I', ' He', She' snd 'It'; and* **'were'** *for pronouns 'You', 'We', ' They' as shown on the two placards attached to two different branches-compare the figure at the left.*

All the rest of the attributes of this tense are as described for Active past indefinite tense.

Assertive Negative

Form: **Subject + to be +NP +Ven + by + Agent + T.**

I + was + not + seen + by + them + yesterday.

e.g. You + were + not + seen + by + them + yesterday.

He/She/It + was + not + seen + by + them + yesterday.

They + were + not + seen + by + him + yesterday.

Interrogative Positive

Form: **To be+ Subject + Ven + by + Agent + T + ?**

Was + I + seen + by + them + yesterday + ?

e.g. Were + you + seen + by + them + yesterday + ?

Was + he/she/it + seen + by + them + yesterday + ?

Were + they + seen + by + him + yesterday + ?

Interrogative Negative

Form: To be+Subject + NP + Ven + by + Agent + T +?

e.g. Was + I + not + seen + by + them + yesterday +?

Were + you + not + seen + by + them + yesterday+?

Was +he/she/it + not + seen + by + them + yesterday +?

Were + they + not + seen + by + him + yesterday + ?

SHORT FORMS

Note the following short forms of the modal verb with negative particle 'not'.

Assertive Negative

Form: Subject + to be+NP + Ven + by + Agent + T.

e.g. I + wasn't + seen + by + them + yesterday.

You + weren't + seen + by + them + yesterday.

He/She/It + wasn't + seen + by + them + yesterday.

They + weren't + seen + by + him + yesterday.

Interrogative Negative

***Form:* To be+NP+Subject+ Ven + by + Agent + T + ?**

e.g. Wasn't + I + seen + by + them + yesterday + ?

Weren't + you + seen + by + them + yesterday + ?

Wasn't +he/she/it + seen + by + them + yesterday + ?

Weren't + they + seen + by + him + yesterday + ?

❐ ❐ ❐

Passive Voice
Future Indefinite Tense

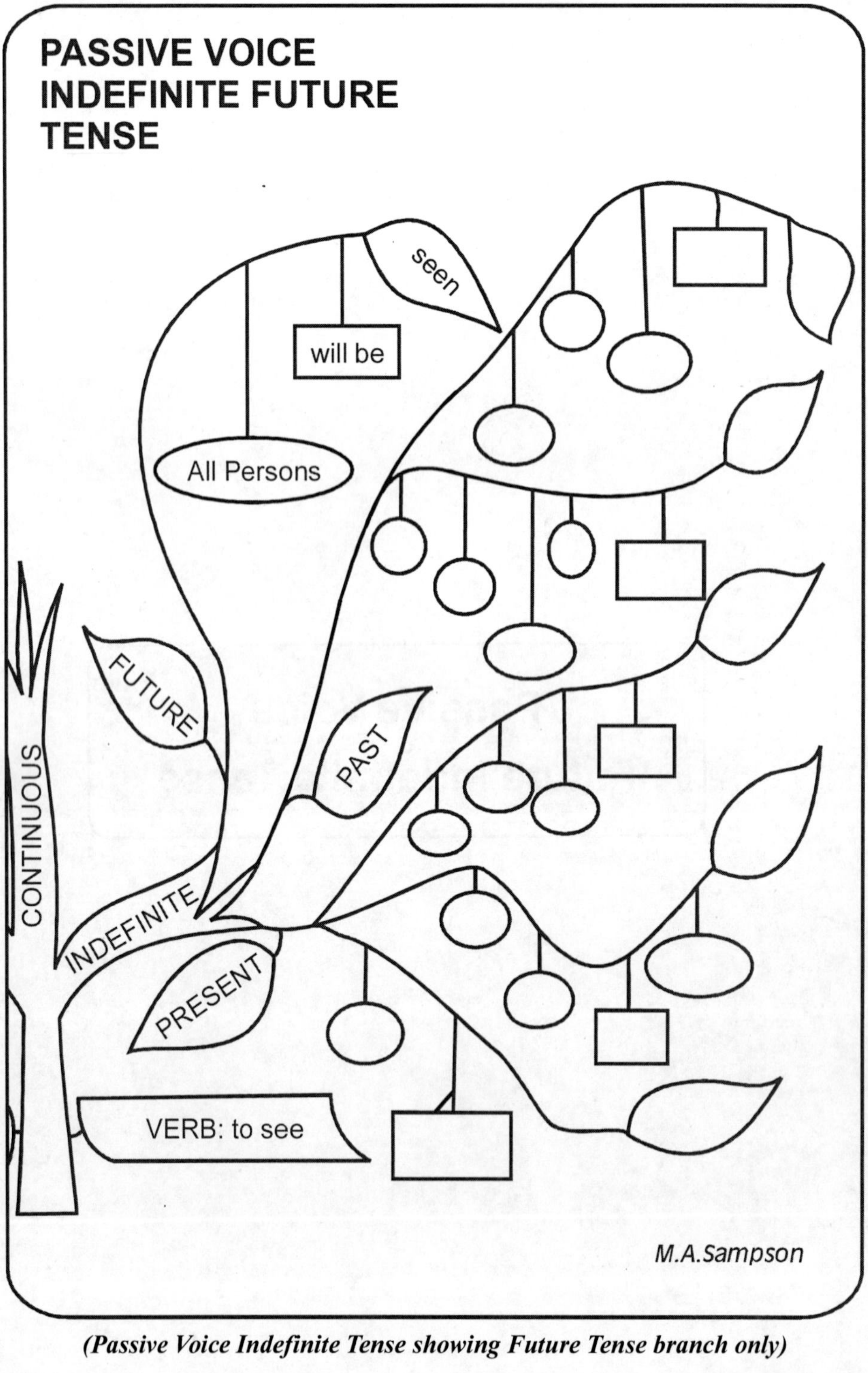

(Passive Voice Indefinite Tense showing Future Tense branch only)

Future Indefinite Tense

Assertive Affirmative

***Form:* Subject + M + to be + Ven + by + Agent + T.**

I/We + shall + be + seen + by + them + tomorrow.

You/He/She/It + will + be + seen + by + them + tomorrow.

In the Future Simple (Indefinite Tense), the verb shows that the event will be completed at a point of time in the future but does not specify exact time when the event is going to take place.***We must have a part of the sentence to show that the event has taken place in the future.*** In the model example 'tomorrow'does that work.If ,however, this part is not given in the sentence of this tense 'any' time in the future from the time of speaking ,is to be taken as understood.

a. A letter will be written by her yesterday.

b. Letters will be written by them two days before.

From the Future Indefinite branch , it can be seen that all the seven personal pronouns take 'will be' placard(board) attached to the branch before the past participle 'seen' is read

*The board (placard) for **'will be'** is split into two **'will'** and **'be'**. In the above form they represent **'M'** (for Modal auxiliary) and for **'to be'**.*

Note ' M' is used for Modal Auxiliary.

Assertive Negative

***Form:* Subject + M + NP + to be + Ven + by + Agent + T.**

I/We + shall + not + be + seen + by + them + tomorrow.

You/He/She/It + will + not + be + seen + by +them + tomorrow.

Interrogative Positive

***Form:* M + Subject + to be + Ven + by +Agent + T + ?**

Shall + I/we + be + seen + by + them + tomorrow + ?

Will +you/he/she/it + be + seen + by +them +tomorrow + ?

Interrogative Negative

Form: **M + Subject + to be + NP + Ven + by + Agent + T +?**

Shall + I/we + to be + not +seen +by + them + tomorrow+ ?

Will + you/he/she/it + be + not + seen + by + them + tomorrow + ?

SHORT FORMS

Note the following short forms of the modal verb with negative particle 'not'.

Assertive Negative

Form: **Subject +M+NP + to be + Ven + by + Agent + T.**

I/We + shan't + be + seen + by + them + tomorrow.

You/He/She/It + won't + be + seen + by + them + tomorrow.

Interrogative Negative

Form: **M+NP +Subject +to be + Ven + by +Agent + T + ?**

Shan't +I/we + be + seen + by + them + tomorrow + ?

Won't +you/he/she/it + be + seen + by + them + tomorrow + ?

❒ ❒ ❒

Passive Voice
Continuous Tenses

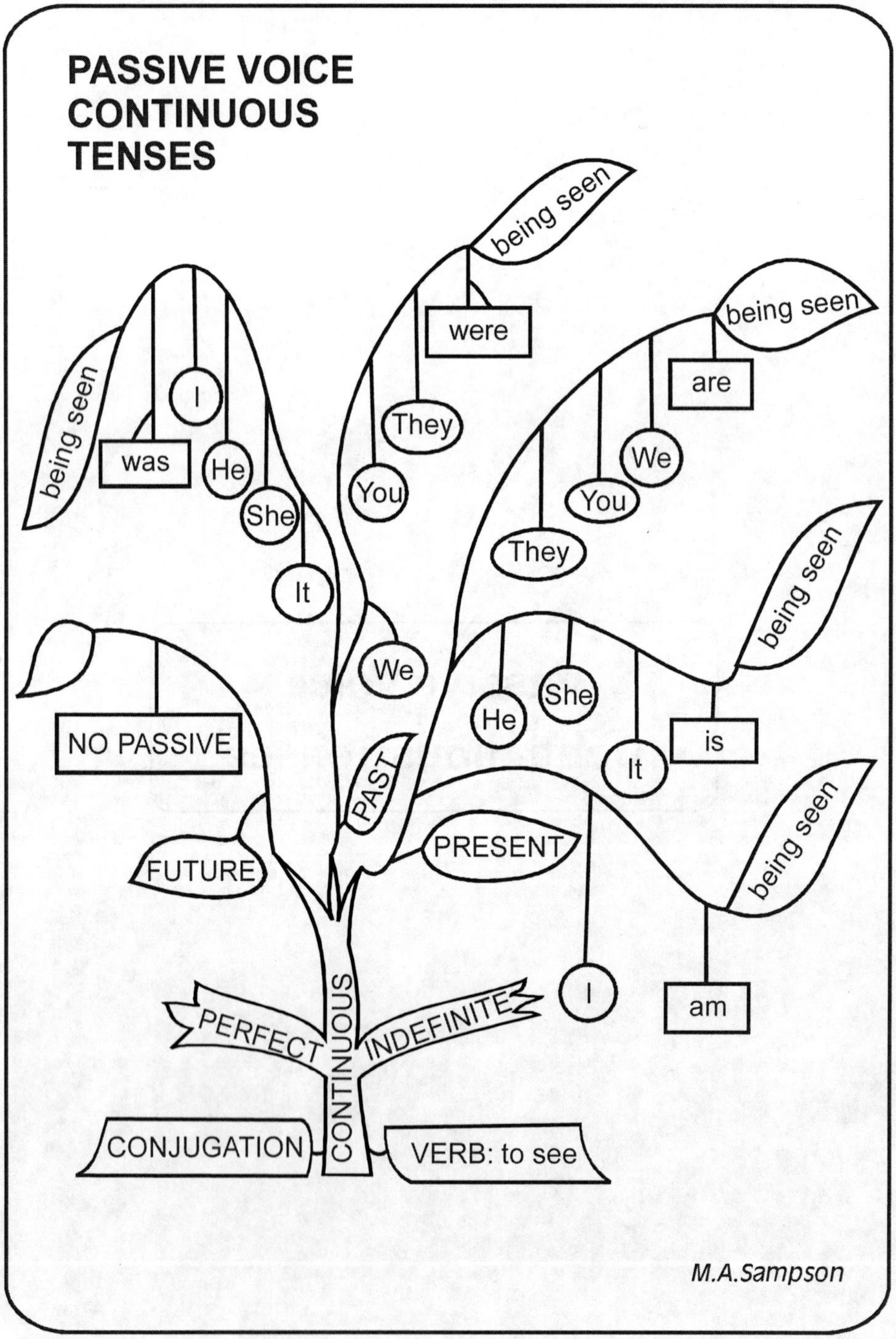

(Passive Voice Continuous Branch showing letters to the Present and Past tense branches only)

Passive Voice

Continuous Branch

Present **Past**

In English Language there is ***no passive voice*** for future tense.

See the adjoining Passive Voice tree branch . You will notice that there is a large placard (board) attached to the future tense branch 'NO PASSIVE'that declares that this branch does not have passive voice equivalent sentence. Heence no past participle shown on the leaf attached to the branch at the end..

Present Continuous

The speech ***is being given*** by the principal of the college now.

A song ***is being sung*** by the monitor ofthe class.

Past Tense

Breafast ***was being taken*** by my friend when I visited him yesterday.

A song ***was being sung*** yesterday when I entered the hall.

Note: There is no future continuous for passive voice sentences

SHORT FORMS

to be: am, is , are, was, were

M: Modal Verbs like will should etc.

NP: Negative Particle 'no' and 'not'

S: Subject or Subject Phrase

O: Object or Object Phrase

V: Present Tense form of the verb like go, write etc.

Vs: Present tense form 's' added to it belonging to third person, singular number and present tense e.g. writes, does, goes, is,has etc.

Ving: Present Participle form of the verb like writing, coming, bringing etc.

Ved: Past Tense form of the verb like wrote, sang, pulled, brought etc.

Ven: Past participle form of the verb like written, sung, brought, pulled etc.

T: Time Phrase

All Persons: I,we,;you;he,she,It,they

Passive Voice
Present Continuous Tense

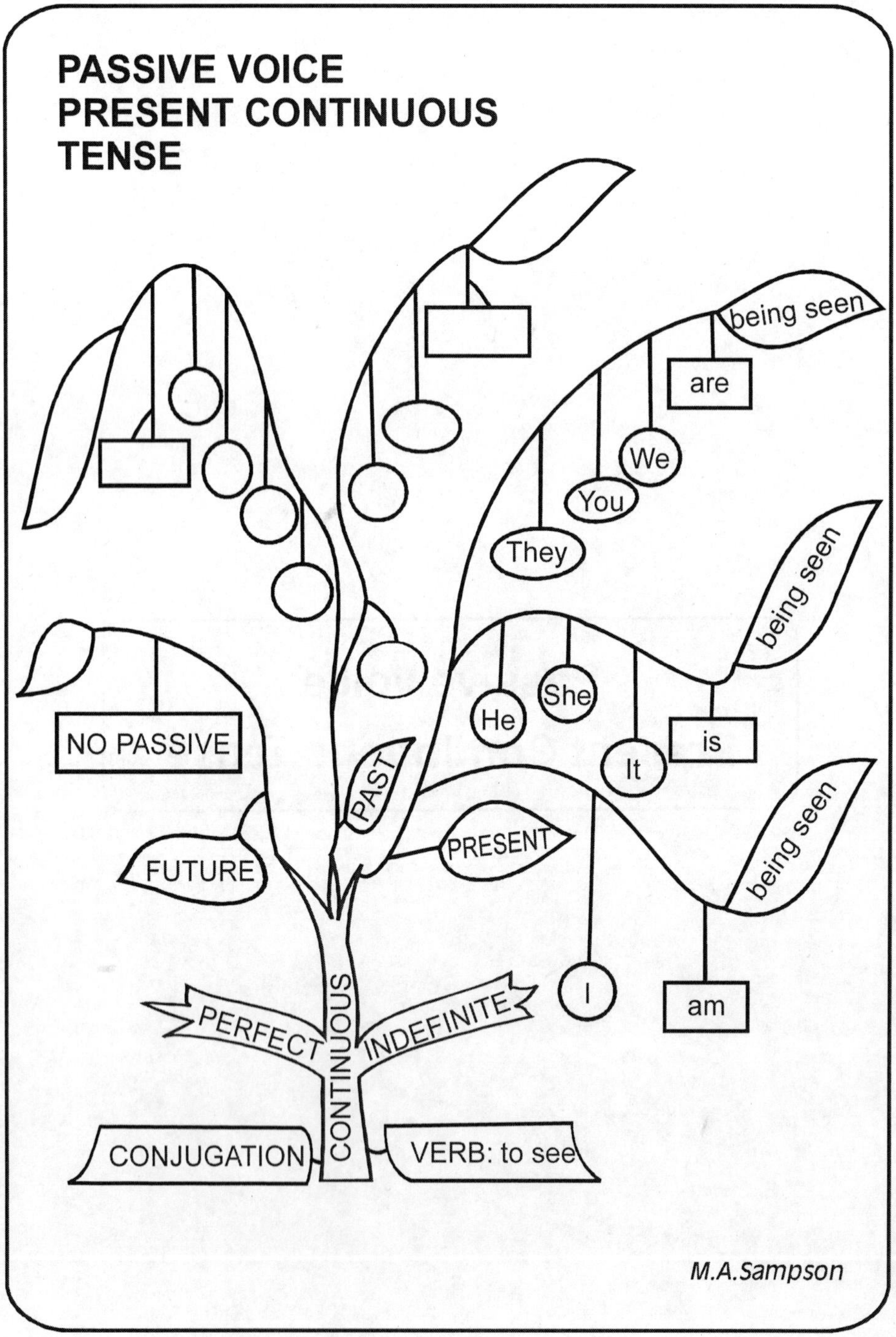

(Passive Voice Continuous Branch showing letters to the Present tense branch only)

Present Continuous Passive Tense

Assertive Affirmative

Form: **Subject + M + to be+Past Part +by + Agent + T.**

e.g. I + am + being + seen + by + them + now.

A letter + is + being + written + by + her + now.

The donkeys + are+ being + beaten + by + the boys + now.

In these Present Continuous Tense the verb shows that the action mentioned in it is continued in the given span of time. This given span of time as the rest of the sentence gives the time sense whether action is in the present or past. Hence the part of the sentence that limits the span of time is essential without which it becomes indefinite sentence in the continuous form. If, however, the part of the sentence that limits the span of time is not given then 'now' is undertood in the present continuous sentences.

There are three auxiliaries, **'am'***,for the pronoun 'I',* **'is'***for pronouns, 'He', She'snd 'It'; and* **'are'***for pronouns 'You', 'We', and ' They'as shown on the three placards attached to three different branches-compare the figure at the left.*

All the rest of the attributes of this tense are as described for Active Voice Present Continuous tenses.

Assertive Negative

Form: **S +M + NP + to be + Ven + by + Agent + T.**

I +am + not + being + seen + by + them + now.

A letter + is + not + being + written + by + her + now.

The dinkeys+are + not + being + beaten + by + the boys + now.

Interrogative Positive

Form: **M +Subject + to be + Ven + by + Agent + T + ?**

Am + I + being + seen + by + them + now + ?

Is + a letter + being + written + by + her + now + ?.

Are+ the dinkeys + being + beaten + by + the boys +now + ?

Interrogative Negative

Form: **M + S + NP + to be +Ven +by + Agent + T +?**

Am + I + not + being + seen +by + them + now +?

Is + a letter + not + being + written+by + her + now +?

Are + the dinkeys + not + being + beaten +by + the boys + now +?

SHORT FORMS

Note the following short forms of the modal verb with negative particle 'not'.

Assertive Negative

Form: **Subject + M+NP + to be + Ven + by + Agent + T.**

I + ain't + being + seen +by + them + now.

A letter + isn't + being + written+by + her + now.

The dinkeys + aren't + being + beaten +by + the boys + now.

Interrogative Negative

Form: **M+NP + Subject + to be + Ven + by + Agent + T + ?**

Ain't + I + being + seen + by + them + now + ?

Isn't + a letter + being + written + by + her + now + ?.

Aren't + the dinkeys+ being + beaten + by + the boys + now + ?

❐ ❐ ❐

Passive Voice
Past Continuous Tense

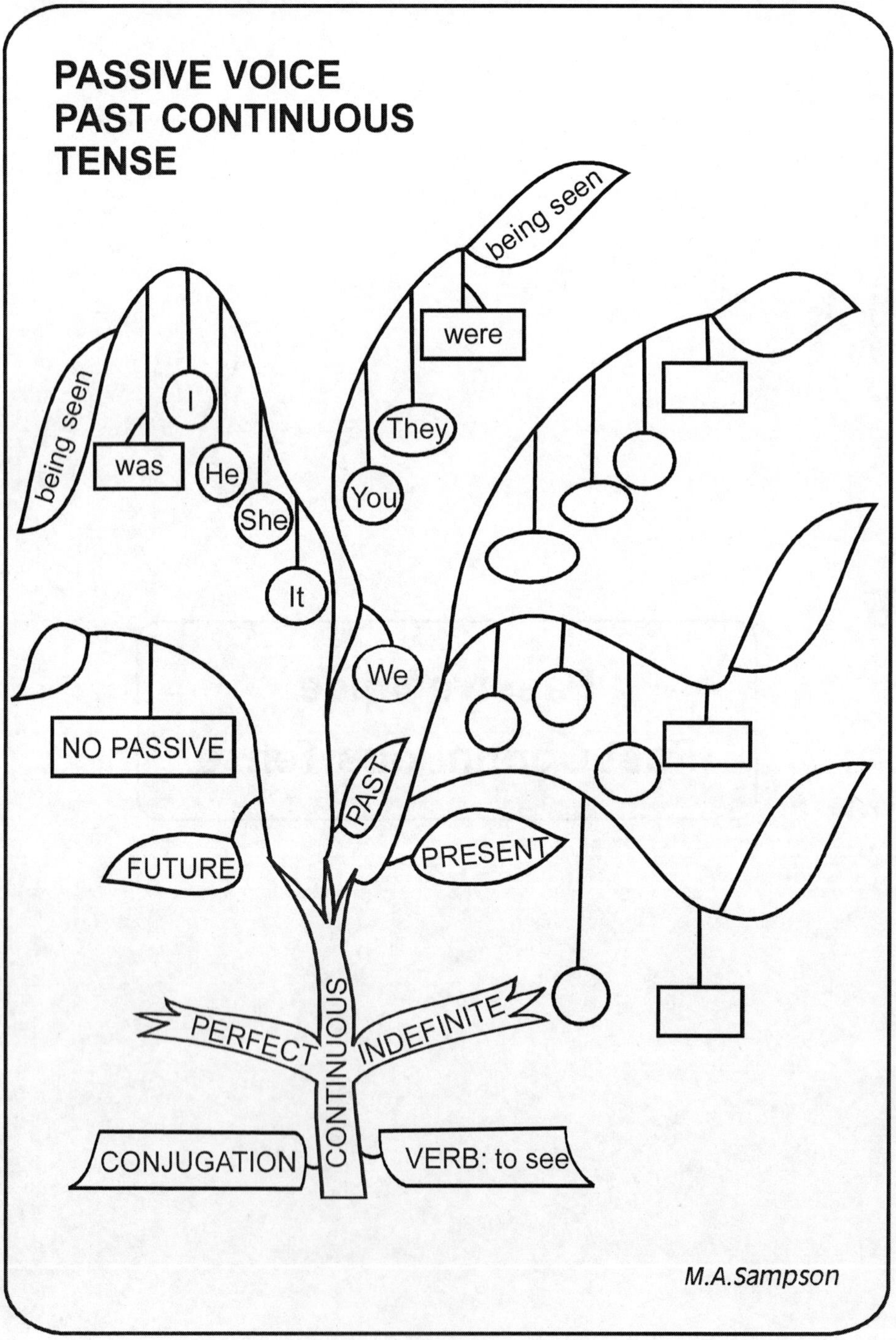

(Passive Voice Continuous Branch showing letters to the Past tense branch only)

Past Continuous Passive Tense

Assertive Affirmative

Form: **Subject + M + to be + Ven + by + Agent + T.**

I + was + being + seen + by + her + yesterday from 9:a.m. to 9:15 a.m.

They + were + being +punished + by + the police + when I saw them yesterday.

In the Past Continuous Tense the verb shows that the action mentioned in it is continued in the given span of time. This given span of time as the rest of the sentence gives the time sense whether the action is in the past,and also limits the time through which the action was going on.It is rediculous to say 'I was being seen by her yesterday' because seeing action cannot go on for 24 hours as the span of time for 'yesterday'is of 24 hours. It, certainly, does not mean 'I was seen by her yesterday' In that case the sentence will be of ' Indefinite' tense and not of 'continuous' tense.

*There are two auxiliaries, '**was**', for the pronouns 'I', 'He', 'She' and 'It'; and '**were**' for pronouns 'You', 'We', and 'They' as shown on the two placards attached to two different branches-Compare the figure at the left.*

All the rest of the attributes of this tense are as described for Active Voice Past Continuous tenses.

Assertive Negative

Form: **S + M + NP+ to be + Ven + by + Agent + T**

I + was + not + being + seen + by + her + yesterday from 9:a.m. to 9:15 a.m.

They + were + not + being + punished + by + the police +when I saw them yesterday.

Interrogative Positive

Form: **M + Subject + to be + Ven + by + Agent + T + ?**

Was + I + being + seen + by + her + yesterday from 9:a.m. to 9:15 a.m + ?

Were + they + being + punished + by + the police + when you saw them yesterday + ?

Interrogative Negative

Form: **M + S + NP + to be + Ven + by + Agent + T + ?**

Was + I + not + being + seen + by + her + yesterday from 9:a.m. to 9:15 a.m+?

Were +they + not + being + punished + by + the police + when I saw them yesterday +?

SHORT FORMS

Note the following short forms of the modal verb with negative particle 'not'.

Assertive Negative

Form: **S + M+NP + to be + Ven + by + Agent + T**

I + wasn't + being + seen + by + her + yesterday from 9:00 a.m. to 9:15 a.m.

S + M+NP + to be + Ven + by + Agent + T.

They+ weren't + being + punished + by + the police + when I saw them yesterday.

Interrogative Negative

Form: **M+NP + Subject + to be + Ven + by + Agent + T+ ?**

Wasn't + I + being + seen + by + her + yesterday from 9:a.m. to 9:15 a.m+?

Weren't + they + being + punished +by + the police + when I saw them yesterday +?

❐ ❐ ❐

For Passive Voice there are No Future Continuous Tense Sentences

SHORT FORMS

to be: am, is , are, was, were

M: Modal Verbs like will should etc.

NP: Negative Particle ‘no’ and ‘not’

S: Subject or Subject Phrase

O: Object or Object Phrase

V: Present Tense form of the verb like go, write etc.

Vs: Present tense form ‘s’ added to it belonging to third person, singular number and present tense e.g. writes, does, goes, is,has etc.

Ving: Present Participle form of the verb like writing, coming, bringing etc.

Ved: Past Tense form of the verb like wrote, sang, pulled, brought etc.

Ven: Past participle form of the verb like written, sung, brought, pulled etc.

T: Time Phrase

All Persons: I,we,;you;he,she,It,they

Passive Voice

Perfect Tense Branch

Present | Past | Future

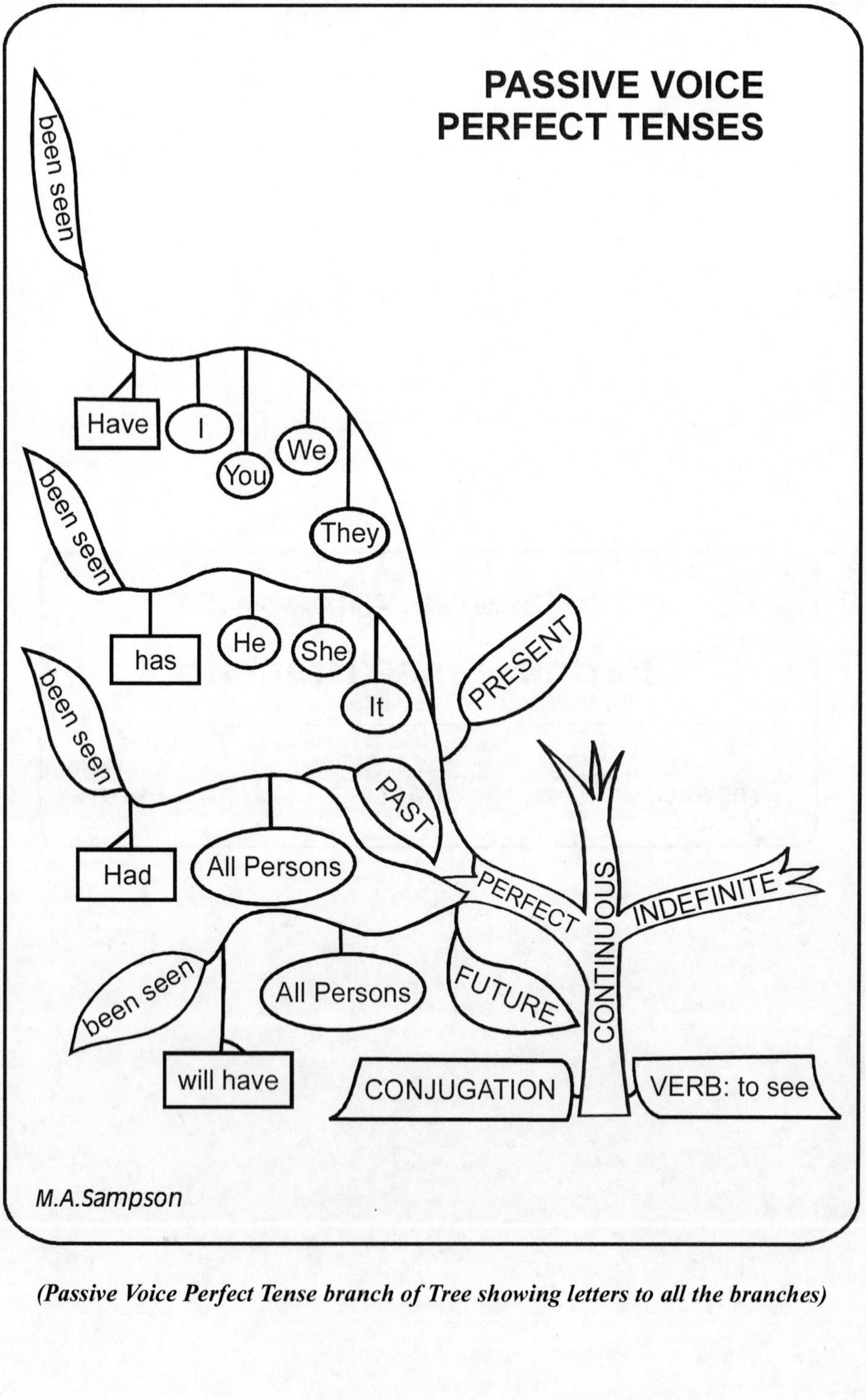

(Passive Voice Perfect Tense branch of Tree showing letters to all the branches)

Passive Voice
Perfect Tense Branch

Present **Past** **Future**

Perfect Tenses are of those sentences which indicate completed activity in the immediate past;an action copleted before a certain moment in the past or completion of the action is going to take place by a certain future time.

Present Tense

A shirt has been woven by me this week.

I have been helped by my friends for mystudies.

Past Tense

A shirt had been woven by me before the function last week.

The donkeys were beaten by the boys to drive them away.

Future Tense

A shirt will have been woven by me by this time next week.

I shall have been helped by my friends to complete the work next week.

SHORT FORMS

to be:	am, is , are, was, were
M:	Modal Verbs like will should etc.
NP:	Negative Particle 'no' and 'not'
S:	Subject or Subject Phrase
O:	Object or Object Phrase
V:	Present Tense form of the verb like go, write etc.
Vs:	Present tense form 's' added to it belonging to third person, singular number and present tense e.g. writes, does, goes, is,has etc.
Ving:	Present Participle form of the verb like writing, coming, bringing etc.
Ved:	Past Tense form of the verb like wrote, sang, pulled, brought etc.
Ven:	Past participle form of the verb like written, sung, brought, pulled etc.
T:	Time Phrase
All Persons:	I,we,;you;he,she,It,they

Passive Voice
Present Perfect Tense

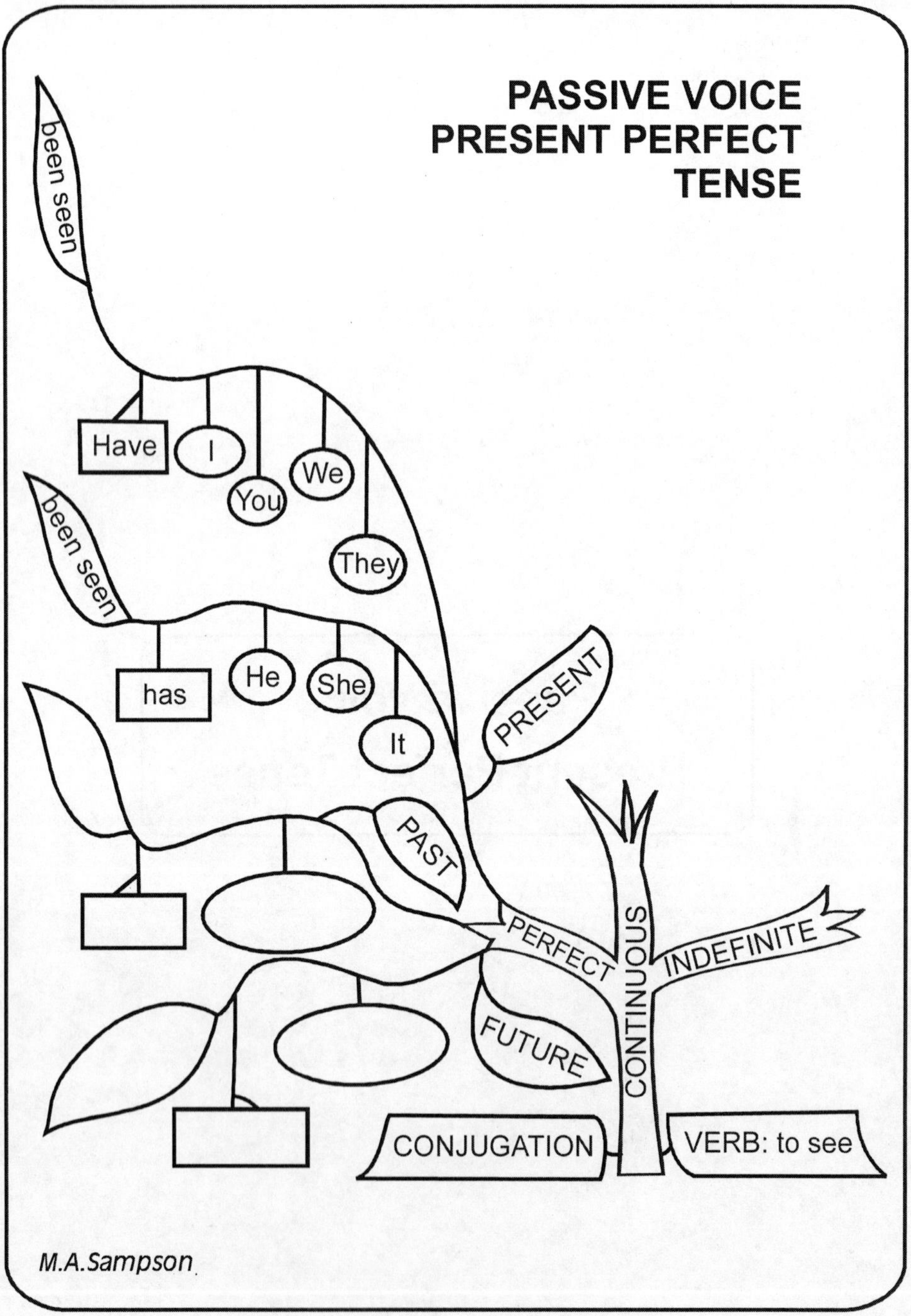

(Passive Voice Perfect Tense showing letters to Present Tense of the branch only)

Present Perfect Passive Tense

Assertive Affirmative

Form: S + M + to be + Ven + by + Agent + T.

I + have + been + seen + by + her + just now

He + has + been + punished + by + the police + just now.

In the Present Perfect Tense the verb shows that the action mentioned in it is cmpleted in the given span of time. This given span of time as the rest of the sentence gives the time sense whether the action is in the Present,and ***also limits*** the time through which the action was completed.

There are two auxiliaries, ' **have** *' for pronouns , 'I', 'We', 'You' and 'They' and '***has***', for the pronouns , 'He', 'She' snd 'It'; as shown on the two placards attached to two different branches in the adjoining figure-Compare.*

All the rest of the attributes of this tense are as described for Active Voice of Present Perfect tenses.

Assertive Negative

***Form:* S + M + NP + to be + Ven + by + Agent + T**

I +have+ not + been + seen + by + her + just now.

He+ has + not + been + punished + by + the police + just now.

Interrogative Positive

***Form:* M + S + to be + Ven + by + Agent + T + ?**

Have + I + been + seen + by + her + just now + ?

Has + he +been + punished + by + the police + just now + ?

Interrogative Negative

***Form:* M + S + NP + to be + Ven + by + Agent + T + ?**

Have + I + not + been + seen + by + her + just now +?

Has + he+ not + been + punished + by + the police + just now +?

SHORT FORMS

Note the following short forms of the modal verb with negative particle 'not'.

Assertive Negative

Form: **S + M+NP + to be + Ven + by + Agent + T.**

I + haven't + been + seen + by + her + just now

He + hasn't + been + punished + by + the police + just now.

Interrogative Negative

Form: **M+NP + S + to be + Ven + by + Agent + T + ?**

Haven't + I + been + seen + by + her + just now + ?

Hasn't + he + been + punished + by + the police + just now + ?

Exercise 1

Put the verbs in the brackets into the Present Perfect Continuous tense:

1. She _______ (overwork). That is why she looks so tired.
2. There will be a flood soon because it _____ (rain) for two days now.
3. You _______ (drive) whole day. Let me drive now.
4. I feel irritable because I ______ (not eat) enough lately.
5. It ______ (snow) for three days now.
6. I ______ (live) here since 1995.
7. The Minister ______ (speak) for an hour now.
8. How long you _______ (wear) glasses?

9. Someone _______ (use) my computer.

10. We ______ (look) forward to this holiday for months

11. John <u>has worked</u> in Washington <u>for three years.</u>

    OR

12. John <u>has been working</u> in Washington <u>for three years.</u>

SHORT FORMS

to be:	am, is , are, was, were
M:	Modal Verbs like will should etc.
NP:	Negative Particle 'no' and 'not'
S:	Subject or Subject Phrase
O:	Object or Object Phrase
V:	Present Tense form of the verb like go, write etc.
Vs:	Present tense form 's' added to it belonging to third person, singular number and present tense e.g. writes, does, goes, is,has etc.
Ving:	Present Participle form of the verb like writing, coming, bringing etc.
Ved:	Past Tense form of the verb like wrote, sang, pulled, brought etc.
Ven:	Past participle form of the verb like written, sung, brought, pulled etc.
T:	Time Phrase
All Persons:	I,we,;you;he,she,It,they

Passive Voice
Past Perfect Tense

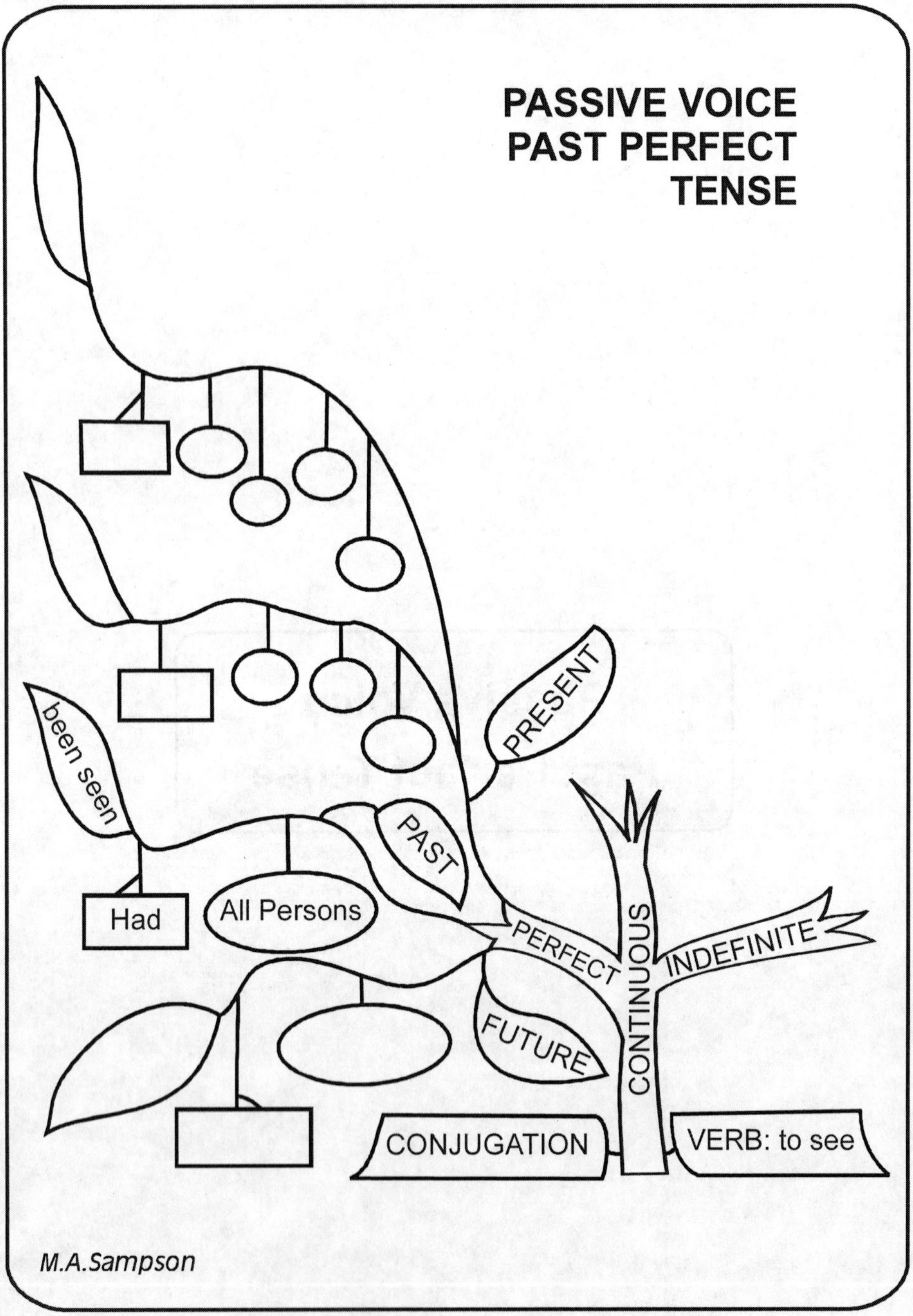

(Passive Voice Perfect Tense showing letters to Past Tense of the branch only)

Past Perfect Passive Tense

Assertive Affirmative

Form: **S + M + to be + Ven + by + Agent + T.**

I + had + been + seen + by + her + before others did.

He + had + been +punished+ by +the police+before leaving him.

In the Past Perfect Tense the verb shows that the *action was completed before something completed.* **Hence it is rightly called as the tense with double past finite verb. This sentence necessarily has two clauses either explicitely given or one of them is implied.** One clause is a perfect tense clause and other one is past indefinite clause.

There is only one Modal auxiliary(had) for all the seven personal pronoun. Hence only one branch is shown with one Placard written 'had' on it.

All the rest of the attributes of this tense are as described for Active Voice Past Perfect tenses.

Assertive Negative

Form: **S + M +NP + to be + Ven + by+Agent + T.**

I + had + not + been + seen + by + her + before others did.

He + had + not + been +punished +by + the police + before leaving him.

Interrogative Positive

Form: **M + S + to be + Ven + by + Agent + T + ?**

Had + I + been + seen + by + her + before others did + ?

Had + he + been +punished +by+ the police + before leaving him + ?

Interrogative Negative

Form: **M + S + NP + to be + Ven + by + Agent + T + ?**

Had + I + not +been +seen + by + her +before others did + ?

Had + he + not + been + punished + by + the police + before leaving him + ?

SHORT FORMS

Note the following short forms of the modal verb with negative particle 'not'.

Assertive Negative

Form: S + M+NP + to be + Ven + by +Agent+ T

I + hadn't + been + seen + by + her + before others did.

He+ hadn't + been + punished + by + the police + before leaving him.

Interrogative Negative

***Form:* M + NP +S +to be + Ven + by +Agent + T + ?**

Hadn't + I + been + seen + by + her + before others did + ?

Hadn't + he + been + punished + by + the police + before leaving him + ?

This past perfect concept can also be conveyed by the past perfect continuous tense. Study the following rule.

subject + had + been + [verb + ing]....

Abdul had been living in New York for ten years before he moved to California.

Examples of past perfect:

The professor had reviewed the material before he gave the quiz. After Henry had visited Puerto Rico, he went to St. Thomas. Before Ali went of sleep, he had called his family.

George had worked at the university for forty-five years before he retired.

OR

George had been working at the university for forty-five years before he retired.

After the committee members had considered the consequences, they voted on the proposal.

The doctor had examined the patient thoroughly before he prescribed the medication.

❐ ❐ ❐

Passive Voice
Future Perfect Tense

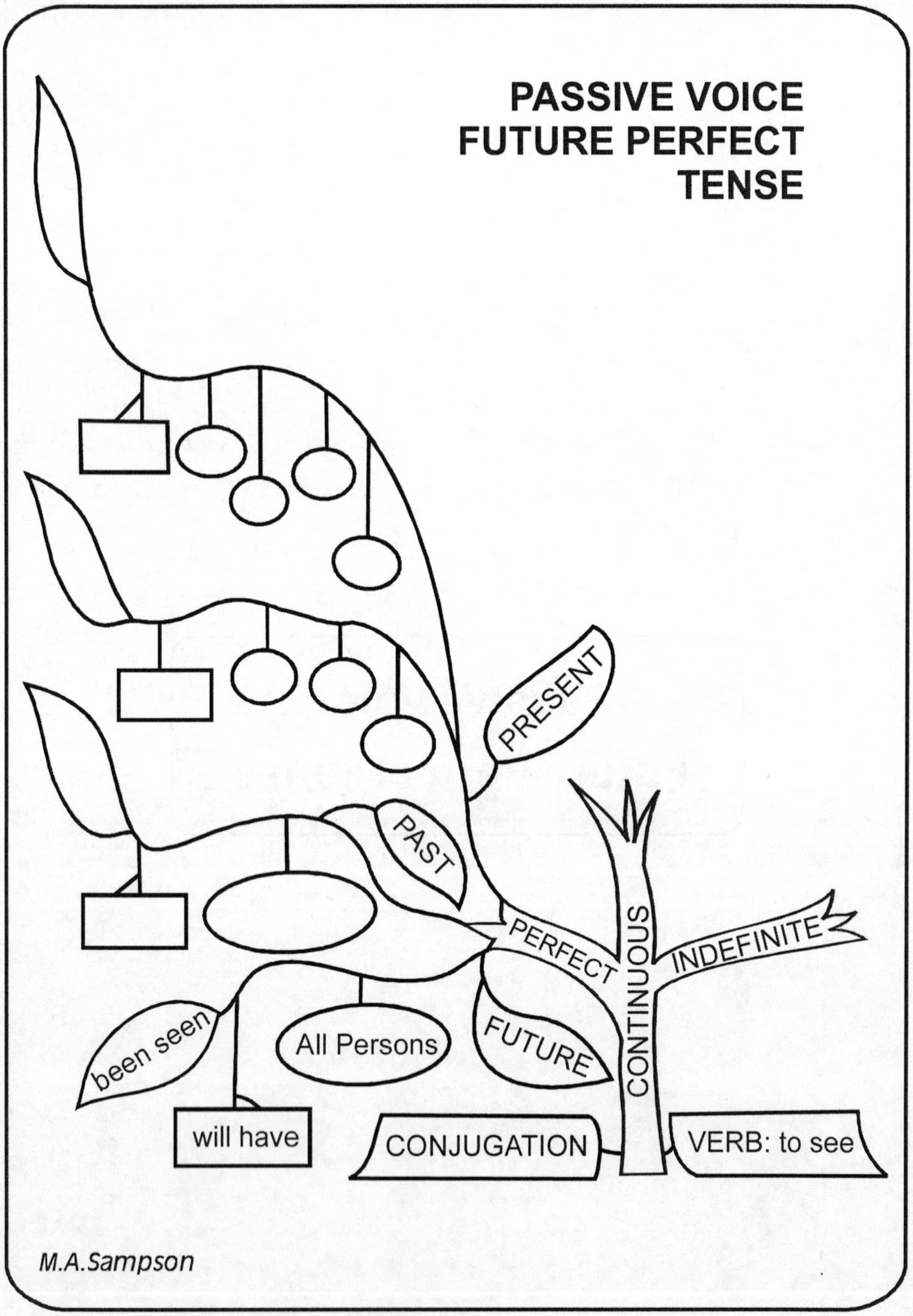

(Passive Voice Perfect Tense showing letters to Future Tense of the branch only)

Future Perfect Passive Tense

Assertive Affirmative

Form: **S + M + have + to be +Ven + by + Agent + T.**

I + will + have + been + seen + by + her + tomorrow by this time.

She + will + have + been + seen + by + him + tomorrow by this time.

All the personal pronouns have the same structure for this tense. Hence only one branch with the placard 'will have' is shown in the figure.

In the Future Perfect Tense the verb shows that the action is going to be completed by the point of a time and this point is in the future. Hence it also has two finite verbs in the sentence which necessarily mean that there are two clauses both of future tense. However one is of perfect tense and other one is of simple tense. Both the clauses are either explicitly given or one of them is implied.The explicite clause is invariably of future perfect tense.

There compound Modal auxiliary(will have) is for all the seven personal pronouns. Hence only one branch is shown with one Placard with 'will have' on it.

All the rest of the attributes of this tense are as described for Active Voice future Perfect tenses.

Assertive Negative

Form: **S + M + have + NP + to be + Ven + by +Agent + T**

I + shall + have + not + been + seen + by+ her + tomorrow by this time.

She + will + have + not +been + seen + by + him + tomorrow by this time.

Interrogative Positive

***Form*:M + S + have+ to be + Ven+ by + Agent + T + ?**

Shall +I + have + been +seen + by + her +tomorrow by this time + ?

Will+she+ have+ been +seen + by + him + tomorrow by this time + ?

Interrogative Negative

Form: **M +S + have + NP + to be + Ven + by + Agent + T + ?**

Shall+ I + have + not + been + seen + by + her + tomorrow by this time + ?

Will + she + have + not + been + seen + by + him + tomorrow by this time + ?

SHORT FORMS

Note the following short forms of the modal verb with negative particle 'not'.

Assertive Negative

Form: **S +M+NP + have + to be + Ven + by + Agent + T.**

I + shan't + have + been +seen + by + her + tomorrow by this time.

She +won't + have + been seen +by+him+tomorrow by this time.

Interrogative Negative

Form: **M +NP +S + have + to be + Ven + by + Agent + T + ?**

Shan't + I + have + been +seen + by + her + tomorrow by this time + ?

Won't + she + have + been + seen +by +him + tomorrow by this time + ?

❑ ❑ ❑

Section - 3
(No Passive Voice)
Perfect Continuous Tenses

SHORT FORMS

to be:	am, is , are, was, were
M:	Modal Verbs like will should etc.
NP:	Negative Particle 'no' and 'not'
S:	Subject or Subject Phrase
O:	Object or Object Phrase
V:	Present Tense form of the verb like go, write etc.
Vs:	Present tense form 's' added to it belonging to third person, singular number and present tense e.g. writes, does, goes, is,has etc.
Ving:	Present Participle form of the verb like writing, coming, bringing etc.
Ved:	Past Tense form of the verb like wrote, sang, pulled, brought etc.
Ven:	Past participle form of the verb like written, sung, brought, pulled etc.
T:	Time Phrase
All Persons:	I,we,;you;he,she,It,they

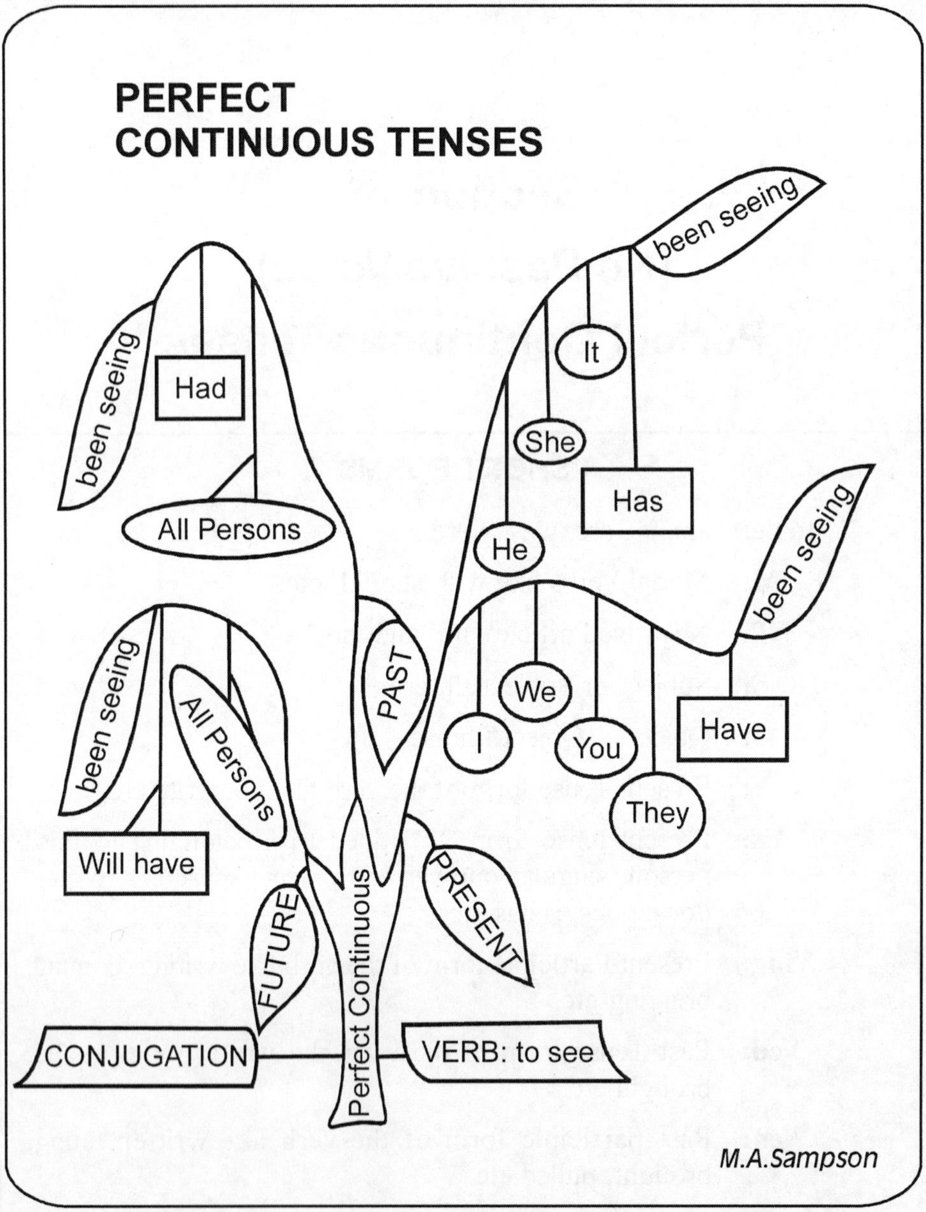

(Perfect Continuous Branch of the Tense Tree showing letters to all the branches)

Perfect Continuous Tenses

Present **Past** **Future**

These tenses do not have their passive equivalents.They also have three kinds of tenses.1. Preseent ,2.Past,and 3. Future

1. **Present Perfect Continuous**

   e.g. The child has been sleeping for two hours.

2. **Past perfect Continuous**

   e.g. We had not been living in this locality since 1996.

3. **Future Perfect Continuous**

   e.g. We shall have been playing since morning.

It is noticed by above sentences that there are two important aspects to these sentences. 1.There is ***a point of time*** and 2. ***action*** stated in the finite verbs ***is still continuing*** either before or after that point of time.

❑ ❑ ❑

SHORT FORMS

to be:	am, is , are, was, were
M:	Modal Verbs like will should etc.
NP:	Negative Particle 'no' and 'not'
S:	Subject or Subject Phrase
O:	Object or Object Phrase
V:	Present Tense form of the verb like go, write etc.
Vs:	Present tense form 's' added to it belonging to third person, singular number and present tense e.g. writes, does, goes, is, has etc.
Ving:	Present Participle form of the verb like writing, coming, bringing etc.
Ven:	Past participle form of the verb like written, sung, brought, pulled etc.
T:	Time Phrase
All Persons:	I,we,;you;he,she,It,they

Present Perfect Continuous Tense

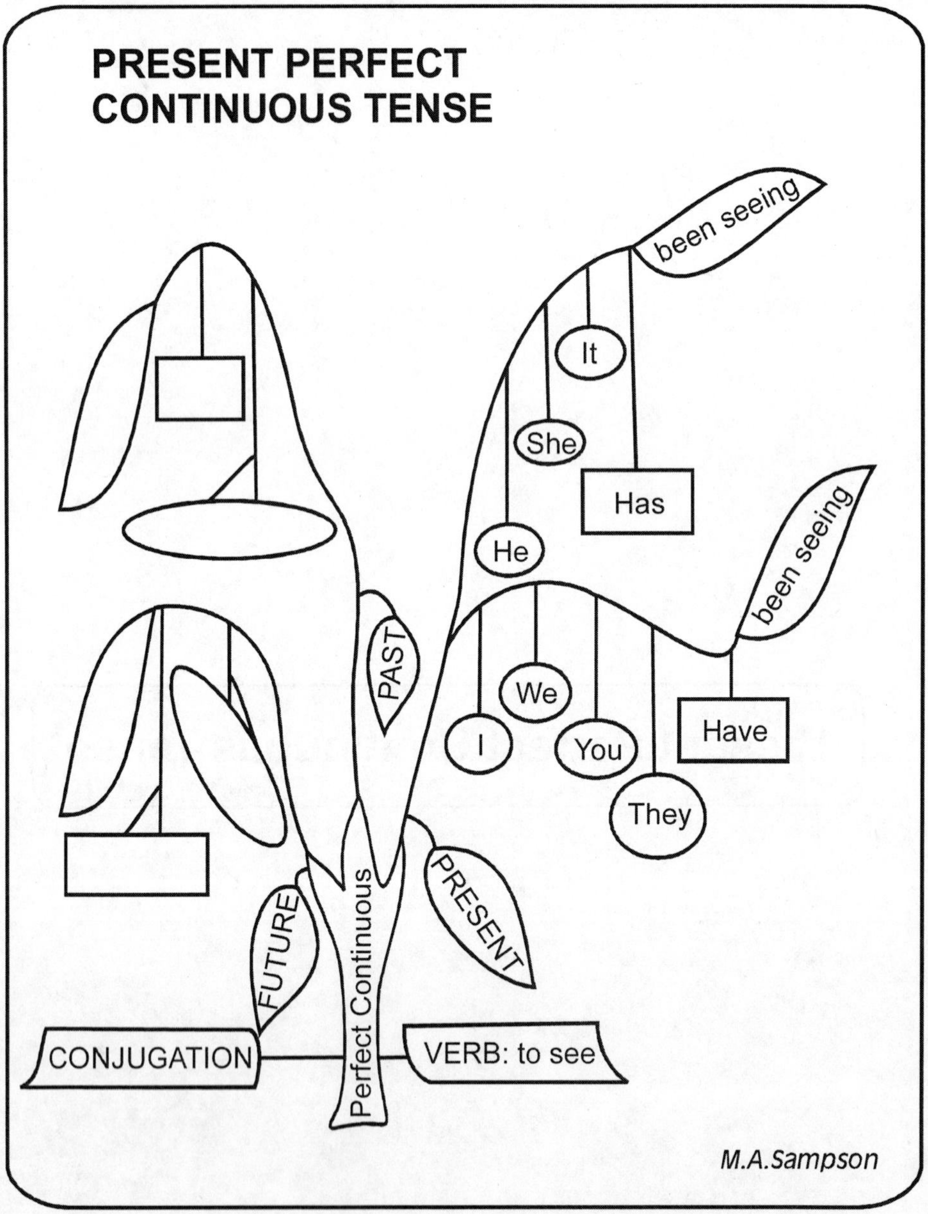

(Perfect Continuous Tense Tree showing letters to Present Tense branch only)

Present Perfect Continuous Tense

Assertive Affirmative

***Form*: S + M + to be+ Ving + Rest (Object,Adverb etc.)**

Cholera + has + been + raging + in Vasai town.

We + have+ been + drawing + a picture since morning.

The Present Perfect Continuous Tense is used to describe actions in progress at the time of speaking or writing and which have been in progress for sometime(expressed or understood) till then.

Assertive Negative

***Form*: S + M + NP + to be + Ving + T**

Cholera + has + not + been + raging + in Vasai town.

We + have + not + been + drawing + a picture since morning.

Interrogative Positive

***Form*: M + S + to be + Ving + rest + ?**

Have + you + been +drawing + a picture since morning + ?

Interrogative Negative

***Form*: M + S + NP +to be + Ving + (O) + rest + ?**

Has + Cholera + not + been + raging + in Vasai town ?

Have +we + not + been + drawing +a picture + since morning + ?

<u>**SHORT FORMS**</u>

Note the following short forms of the modal verb with negative particle 'not'.

Assertive Negative

***Form*: S + M + NP + to be + Ving + rest**

Cholera + hasn't + been + raging + in Vasai town.

We + haven't + been + drawing a picture since morning.

Interrogative Negative

Form: **M + NP + S + to be + Ving + rest + ?**

Hasn't + Cholera + been + raging + in Vasai town + ?

Haven't + we + been +drawing + a picture since morning + ?

USES OF PRESENT PERFECT CONTINUOUS TENSE IS AS FOLLOWS:

1. **Linking the past with the present:**

   The Present Perfect Continuous Tense is used to show that the action that began in the past is continuing up to the present time; as:

   I **have been working** *in the office for ten years.*

2. **Repeated actions:**

   The Present Perfect Continuous expresses a repeated or an uninterrupted action. This tense is not used when we mention the number of times a thing has been done; as

   a. *I* have been asking *him to help me. He refused to help.*

      (I have been asking - *Present Perfect Continous)*

   b. *I* have asked *him five times to help me. He did not help.*

      (I have asked - *Present Perfect Tense)*

3. **Drawing conclusions:**

   The Present Perfect Continuous is used for drawing conclusions based on some evidences; as,

   a. *Nina's eyes are red. It is obvious, she has been* crying.

   b. *Amit has a heavy cold; he* has been studying *late at night.*

For ***an action that began in the past and still occurring in the present*** (present perfect rules, third item), it is also possible to use the present perfect progressive (continuous). Use the following rule to form this aspect.

Subject + {has}	+ been +	[verb + ing]..	
{have}			

John has been living in the same house for twenty years = John has lived in the same house for twenty years and he still continues to live.

❒ ❒ ❒

Past Perfect Continuous Tense

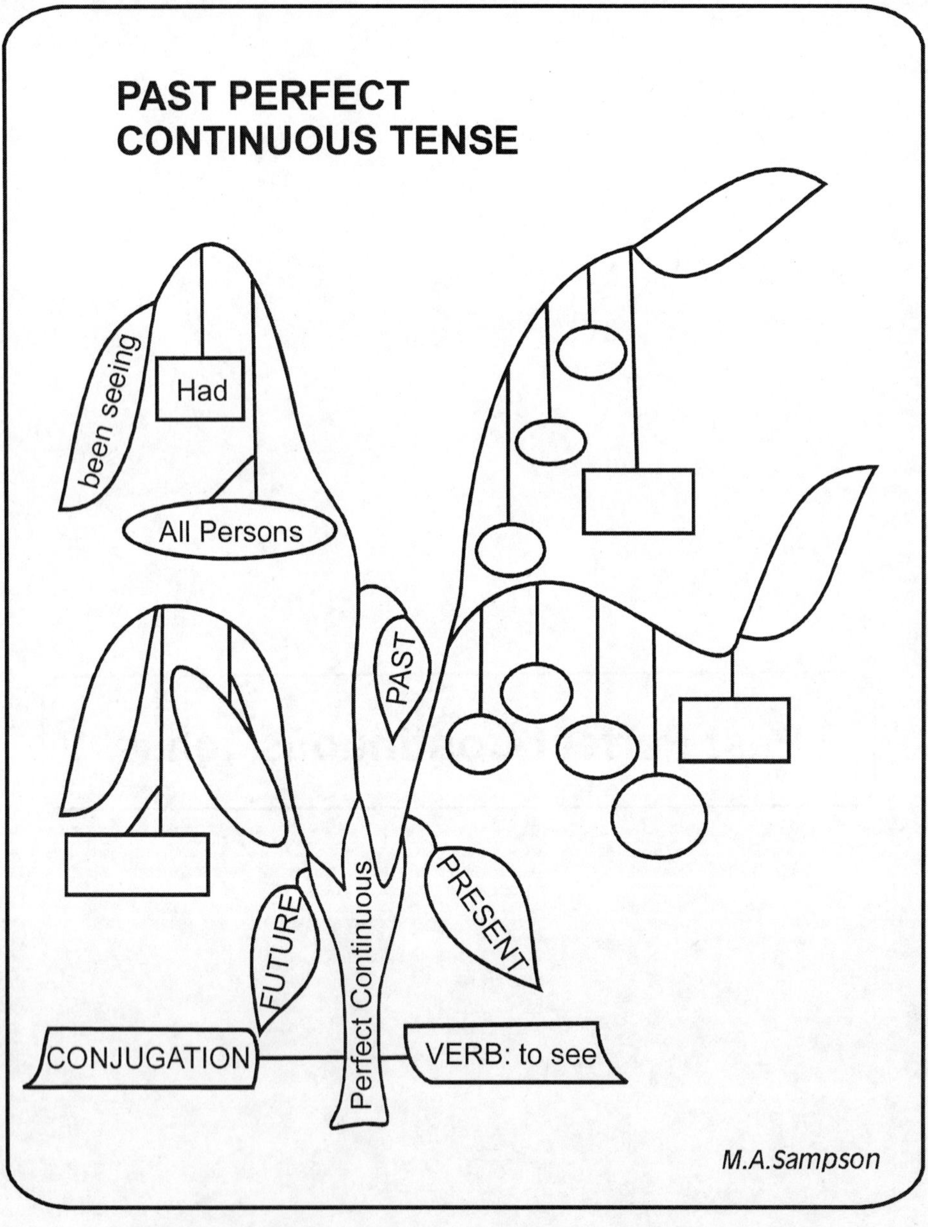

(Perfect Continuous Tense Tree showing letters to Past Tense branch only)

Past Perfect Continuous Tense

Assertive Affirmative

***Form*: S + M + been + Ving + Object + Rest.**

He+had+been + writing + a letter + when I saw her yesterday.

She+had+been + singing + a song + when I entered the hall.

They+had+been + digging + a hole + before taking permission.

The Past Perfect Continuous is used for an action that began before a certain point in the Past and continued upto that time.

e.g. (a) When she came to meet me in December 1990, I had already been awaiting her for three years.

(b) At that time, we had been practising for two years.

(c) They had been building that bridge since 1990.

Note: The preposition used is always "Since" or "for"

Since - denotes a particular point of time.

For - denotes a period of time.

Since 1990

Since last Monday.

For two years.

For two days etc

Assertive Negative

***Form*: S + M + NP + to be + Ving +Object + Rest.**

He+had + not +been+ writing+a letter+when I saw her yesterday.

She + had + not +been + singing + a song + before I entered the hall.

They + had + not + been +digging + a hole + before taking permission.

Interrogative Positive

Form: **M + S + been+ Ving +Object + Rest ?**

Had + he +been + writing + a letter +when I saw her yesterday ?

Had + she +been +singing + a song +before I entered the hall ?

Had + they +been +digging + a hole +before taking permission?

Interrogative Negative

Form: **M + S +NP + been + Ving + Object +Rest?**

Had + he + not + been + writing + a letter + when I saw her yesterday ?

Had + she +not + been + singing +a song + before I entered the hall ?

Had + they + not + been + digging + a hole + before taking permission ?

SHORT FORMS

Note the following short forms of the modal verb with negative particle 'not'.

Assertive Negative

Form: **S + M+NP + been + Ving + Object + Rest.**

He + hadn't + been + writing + a letter + when I saw her yesterday.

She + hadn't +been + singing + a song + before I entered the hall.

They + hadn't +been + digging + a hole + before taking permission.

Interrogative Negative

Form: **M + NP + S + been + Ving + object + Rest?**

Hadn't + he + been + writing + a letter + when I saw her yesterday?

Hadn't + she + been + singing + a song before I entered the hall ?

Hadn't + they + been + digging + a hole + before taking pemrmission?

Past Perfect Continuous Tense is Used for,

1. Time and Duration

The Past Perfect Continuous tense is used to emphasize the time and duration of a continuous activity which took place before a particular time in the past; as:

(a) *The President came back from Tokyo where he* had been meeting *other world leaders.*

(The President had been meeting the world leaders over a period of time; tehn he came back.

(b) *The doctor was very tired because he* had been working *alone.*

2. Drawing Conclusions

The Past Perfect Continuous can be used to show the conclusion (of an action) based on evidence; as

(a) *Amit looked tired. He* had been working *late at night.*

(b) *Seema was fresh because she* had been resting *the whole day.*

3. Repeated Actions

The Past Perfect Continuous is used to show that an action was frequently reapeated; as,

(a) *The teacher was angry because Ravi* had not been doing *his work for a whole week.*

(b) *Joe was annoyed. John* had been phoning *him every day.*

❑ ❑ ❑

SHORT FORMS

to be:	am, is , are, was, were
M:	Modal Verbs like will should etc.
NP:	Negative Particle 'no' and 'not'
S:	Subject or Subject Phrase
O:	Object or Object Phrase
V:	Present Tense form of the verb like go, write etc.
Vs:	Present tense form 's' added to it belonging to third person, singular number and present tense e.g. writes, does, goes, is, has etc.
Ving:	Present Participle form of the verb like writing, coming, bringing etc.
Ven:	Past participle form of the verb like written, sung, brought, pulled etc.
T:	Time Phrase
All Persons:	I,we,;you;he,she,It,they

Future Perfect Continuous Tense

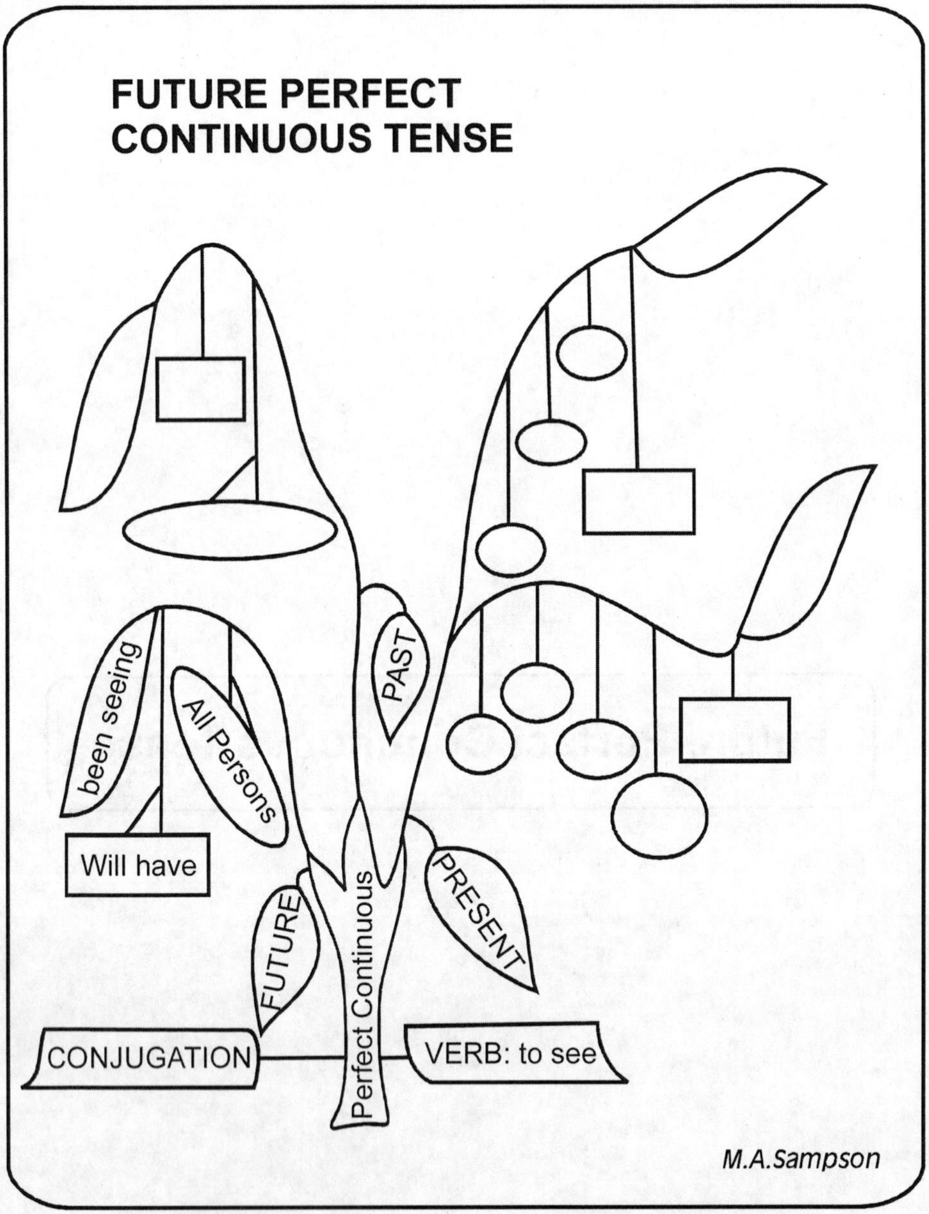

(Perfect Continuous Tense Tree showing letters to Future Tense branch only)

Future Perfect Continuous Tense

Assertive Affirmative

Form: S + M + have+ to be + Ving +(Object) + Rest.

I +shall + have + been + writing + a letter + tomorrow by this time.

She + will + have + been + singing + a song + when I see her at nine in the evening.

They+will +have + been + working + by this date next month.

The future perfect continuous tense shows an action going on over a period of time that will end in the future.

e.g. *1. When he gets his degree, he will have been studying in Cambridge for four years.*

2. By next week, we shall have been doing this job for six weeks.

3. By 1980, she will have been in a large firm..

If you want to indicate the duration of an event at a specific time in the future, you can use the Future Perfect Continuous; as

(a) By March 1998, he *will have been working* for this organization for twelve years.

(b) I *shall have been writing* for half an hour when this lesson ends.

(c) She *will have been learning* dance for five years by March this year.

Assertive Negative

Form:

S + M+NP + have + to be + Ving + Object + Rest.

I + shall+not + have + been + writing + a letter + tomorrow by this time.

She + will+ not + have + been + singing + a song + when I see her at nine in the evening.

They+will+ not + have + been + working + by this date next month.

Interrogative Positive

Form: **Modal + S + have + to be + Ving +(Object) + Rest +?**

Shall + I + have + been +writing + a letter + tomorrow by this time+?

Will + she + have + been +singing + a song + when I see her at nine in the evening + ?

Will + they + have + been +working + by this date next month +?

Interrogative Negative

Form: **M + S+NP + have + to be + Ving +Object + Rest +?**

Shall + I+ not + have + been + writing +a letter + tomorrow by this time + ?

Will + she + not +have + been + singing + a song + when I see her at nine in the evening + ?

Will + they + not + have + been + working + by this date next month + ?

SHORT FORMS

Note the following short forms of the modal verb with negative particle 'not'.

Assertive Negative

Form: **S + M +NP+ have + to be + Ving +(Object)+ Rest.**

I + shan't + have + been + writing + a letter + tomorrow by this time.

She +won't + have + been + singing + a song + when I see her at nine in the evening.

They+won't + have + been + working + by this date next month.

Interrogative Negative

Form: **M+NP + S +have +to be+ Ving +(Object) + Rest + ?**

Shan't + I +have + been + writing + a letter + tomorrow by this time + ?

Won't + she + have + been + singing + a song + when I see her at nine in the evening + ?

Won't + they +have + been + working + by this date next month+?

Miscellaneous Exercises

Exercise

Fill in the blanks using the **Simple Present or the Present Continuous Tense** of the verbs given in bracket:

1. 'Where _______ you _______ now?' 'I ______ to the theatre'. (go)

2. Mr. Gupta ______ (teach) us English everyday. He is absent; so Mr. Kumar _____ (take) our class just now.

3. The sun _______ (rises) in the east.

4. The cock ______ (crow) before dawn every day; but why _____ it ______ (crow) now at ten o'clock.

5. She generally ______ a red skirt but today she ____ a green one. (wear)

6. I ______ (drink) at least six glasses of water every morning.

7. When water ______ (freeze), it ______ (change) into ice.

8. I _______ (practise) speaking Russian everyday.

9. He usually ______ (walk) from his home to the school but today he _____ (go) by car.

10. Look! Someone _______ (knock) at the door.

11. The man who ______ (talk) to Ravi at the moment _____ (speak) eight languages.

❒ ❒ ❒

Exercise: Simple Present and Present Continuous:

Choose either the simple present or present Continuous in the following sentences:

1. Something ______ (smell) very good.
2. We ______ (eat) dinner at seven o'clock tonight.
3. He ______ practice) the piano everyday.
4. They ______ (drive) to school tomorrow.
5. I ______ (believe) you.
6. Maria ______ (have) a cold.
7. Jorge ______ (swim) right now.
8. John ______ (hate) smoke.
9. Jill always ______ (get) up at 6.00 a.m.
10.. 'I _____ at home.' (stay)
11. 'What ______ you ______ this evening?' (do)
12. Ali ______ (do) his homework now. He usually _____ (do) it at night.
13. Where ______ you ______ to spend you holidays this winter? (go)
14. It _____ heavily now. It usually ____ in June. (rain)
15. My friend ______ (come) to visit me next month.
16. Ravi ______ his home work now. He usually _____ it at night. (do)
17. He _____ asleep while he was driving. (fall)
18. If we ______ at 1.00 we will reach by 8 o'clock (start)

19. I _____ a lot of work today. (do)

20. 'What ______ you ______ this evening?' (do) 'I _____ at home.' (stay)

21. Ali ______ (do) his homework now. He usually _____ (do) it at night.

22. Where ______ you ______ to spend you holidays this winter? (go)

25. He generally _____ very well but today he _____ very badly.

23. It ______ heavily now.It usually______ in June.(rain)

❐ ❐ ❐

Exercise

Fill in the blanks with the correct tenses of the verbs in brackets. Use the **simple past tense or the past continuous tense:**

1. The phone _____ (ring) while I _____ (have) lunch.
2. Your telegram _____ (come) just as I _____ (leave) my office.
3. As she _______ (get) into the bus it _____ (start) suddenly.
4. Large crowds ______ (wait) at the aerodrome when the President _______. (arrive)
5. They suddenly ______ (realise) that they ______ (travel) in the wrong direction.
6. When Shyam _______ (arrive) home, his sister ______ (listen) to the radio.
7. As Kavita ______ (get) off the bus, she ______ (slip) and _____ (break) her leg.
8. The sun _____ just _____ (be set) when we ____ (reach) home.
9. She just ______ (open) the letter when the wind ____ (blow) it out of her hand.
10. He ______ (plan) to go to Kerala, but he _____ (change) his mind.
11. My cat _______ (walk) along quietly when Rahul's dog attacked her.
12. She _____ (cut) her finger while she ____ (butter) the bread.
13. Vimal ______ (talk) to his boss when I last _____ (see) him.
14. As I ______ (cross) the road I ______ (step) on a banana skin and _____ (fall).
15. She ________ (write) when I _______ (call) on her.

❒ ❒ ❒

Exercise

Use either the **simple past tense or the past continuous** (progressive) in the following sentences as appropriate:

1. Gene _______ (eat) dinner when his friend called.
2. While Maria was cleaning the apartment, her husband ______ (sleep)
3. At three o'clock this morning, Nitin______ (study).
4. When Mark arrived, the Johnsons _______ (have) dinner, but they stopped in order to talk to him.
5. John ________ (go) to France last year.
6. When the teacher _____ (enter) the room, the students were talking.
7. While Joan was writing the report, Henry ______ (look) for more information.
8. We ______ (see) this movie last night.
9. At one time, Mr. Robert_______ (own) this building.
10. Jose ______ (write) a letter to his family when his pencil _____ break.

❑ ❑ ❑

Exercise on **Simple past and continuous tenses.**

Choose the correct alternative from those given:

1. The Headmaster _____ to speak to you. (wants, is wanting, was wanting)

2. I _____ a new bicycle last week. (bought, have bought, had bought)

3. Here are your shoes: I _____ them. (just clean, just cleaned, have just cleaned)

4. It ____ since early morning. (rained, is raining, has been raining)

5. I ____ a lot of work today. (did have done, had done)

6. I ______ something burning. (smell, am smelling, have been smelling)

7. He will explain it to you when he ______ back. (comes, will come, came)

8. She _____ unconscious since four o'clock. (is, was, has been)

9. He used to visit us every week, but he _____ now. (rarely comes, is rarely coming, has rarely come)

10. If he ____ of your marriage, he will be surprised. (hears, will hear, heard)

❐ ❐ ❐

Exercise

Use the **Past Continuous Tense** in the following sentences:

1. It _______ heavily all night. (rain)

2. _______ football yesterday? (they play)

3. I _______, so I missed what he said. (not listen)

4. I ______ whether you could lend me your car. (wonder)

5. He ______ all weekend (garden)

6. _______ when he left? (you still work)

7. ______ when she came to you? (you read)

8. I lived in Patna, when you ______ in Delhi. (live)

9. ______ cricket match all evening? (you play)

10. When he was young, he _____ football. (always play)

❒ ❒ ❒

Exercise on Tenses

Exercise on **Simple past and continuous tenses.**
Choose the correct alternative from those given:

1. Everyday last week my aunt _____ a plate. (breaks, broke, was breaking)

2. I know all about that film because I ____ it twice. (saw, have seen, had seen)

3. My uncle _____ tomorrow. (arrives, has arrived, will have been arriving)

4. I _____ him since we met a year ago. (didn't see, haven't seen, hadn't seen)

5. We ______ our breakfast half an hour ago. (finished, havgeee finished, had finished)

6. She jumped off the bus while it _____. (moved, had moved, was moving)

7. When we went to the cinema, the film ____. (already started, had already started, would already start)

8. When I pay him tomorrow, he ________ everything I owe him. (has received, has been receiving, will have received)

9. Do you think you ____ me somewhere before? (have seen, had seen, were seeing)

10. The town _____ its appearance comepletely since 1960. (is changing, changed, has changed)

More About Past Perfect Tense

Exercises:

Fill in the blanks with the Past or Past Perfect Tense of the Verbs given in the bracket:

1. Last Sunday, we _______ to visit some friends. *(go)*
2. It _____ everyday this week. *(rain)*
3. Ravi _____ on his cellular phone. *(speak)*
4. I ___________ him for a long time. *(know)*
5. We _______ (come) to this house in 1968 and ____ *(live)* here ever since.
6. I _______ the work just now. *(begin)*
7. The work ________ by me just now. *(begin)*
8. Did you think you ________ me somewhere before? *(see)*
9. _______ you ______ hear that Joykumar ______ *(win)* a scholarship?
10. I ____ each other for the past ten years. *(hear)*
11. I _______ that fellow somewhere before. *(see)*
12. I ______ never ______ alcoholic liquor.

1. I _________ him ten years ago. *(see)*
2. We ______ each other for the past ten years. *(know)*

3. _____ you ever_____to New York? (be)

4. We _______ just ________ you that we are not guilty. *(tell)*

5. Achou ______ a new scooter how. *(buy)*

6. I _______ not yet _______ this exercise. *(finish)*

7. They_______ in this town since 1968. *(live)*

8. She _____ in this hospital since last year. *(work)*

9. We ________ not ___ her for a week. *(see)*

10. She ______ out at o'clock, (go) and _____ not yet _____. *(return)*

11. Several books on that subject ____ during the present year. *(appear)*

12. I ______ to her a few days ago *(write)*, but she ___ not ____ yet. *(reply).*

13. A terrible accident _____ at 9 o' clock this morning. *(occur)*

14. I _______ many a young man ruined by drink. *(see)*

15. She _______ for eight hours last night. *(sleep)*

16. She _____ music while she was in Lonbdon. *(study)*

17. I _______ never _____ her lose her temper. *(see).*

18. Mr. Brown _____ out of work for several months. *(be)*

19. I suppose you ______ *(hear)* the latest news _____ Jaykumar _____ *(marry)* Sarojini yesterday.

20. I ______ never ____ a man to die of love. *(know)*.

21.After she ______ breakfast, she went out to play. *(eat)*

22. When I reached the station, the train _______.*(leave)*

23. I _____ my work, before he arrived. *(finish)*

Exercise 1

Supply the **past perfect or simple past** in the following sentences:

1. The policeman read the suspect his rights after he ______ (arrest) him.

2. After John ______ (wash) his clothes, he began to study.

3. George _____ (wait) for one hour before the bus came.

4. Maria _____ (enter) the university after she had graduated from the community college.

5. Jeannette _____ (wash) the pipettes after she had completed the experiment.

6. Jane sent a letter to her university after she ____ (receive) her scholarship check.

7. After the stewardesses had served lunch to the passengers, the ______ (sit) down.

8. The car _____ (flip) ten times before it landed on its roof.

9. We corrected our papers after we _____ (take) the quiz.

10. John _____ (live) in Mimi for one year when his parents came to visit.

Exercise

Supply the **Past Perfect Tense** of the verbs in brackets:

1. I realised that I _____ (take) the wrong decision.

2. She _____ (leave) by the time Mohan arrived.

3. She said that she ____ (see) that movie.

4. He said that he _____ (complete) the poem.

5. He said that he _____ (see) the culprit before.

6. He asked me why I _____ (leave) the party so early.

7. He knw that he _____ (make) a serious mistake.

8. Previously she ____ (be) a very promising candidate.

9. By the time we arrived they _____ (go).

10. It was reported that the police ____ (capture) the culprit.

❐ ❐ ❐

More about Future Perfect Continuous

Exercise

Fill in the blanks using the **Future Perfect** form of the verbs given in the bracket.

1. I am sure that the contractor ____ (complete) the house by summer this year.

2. Two month from now she ____ (take) her final examination.

3. When you are of my age, you _____ (learn) much about life.

4. By this time next year, you ____ (finish) all your assignments.

5. Before she leaves for London, she ______ (see) every show in town.

6. By the end of January, the contract ________ (sign)

7. You ______ (learn) English by the end of this year.

8. By the time you return, I ______ (finish) washing clothes.

9. Probably you ______ (change) your mind by tomorrow.

10. By this time next month all the flowers _____ (fade).

11. I expect that she ______ (change) her mind by this evening.

❑ ❑ ❑

Rewrite using the APPROPRIATE FORM OF THE VERB given in brackets.

1. My father------- for a brisk evening walk. (go)
2. We ----- for Delhi next Monday. (leave)
3. Rita ------ all her problems . (solve)
4. We have ------ for five years now. (live)
5. I ------- a letter to my sister. (write)
6. He ------ his breakfast when I reached . (have)
7. We --- never --- the man before. (have)
8. I --- the minister last week. (see)
9. The college ------- a cricket match next sunday. (play)
10. He said he ---- next day. (come)
11. The letter ------ yesterday. (post)
12. The teaher --- a the naughty boy. (pardon)
13. If you like the book, you ----- it. (buy)
14. She ----- him if he asked her. (marry)
15. He --- president. (elect)
16. I ------ fifty next month. (be)
17. We ------ in London at this time tomorrow. (be)
18. The parents ----- asleep, but the child was awake. (be)
19. Mr. Timmons -------- in this school for ten years . (teach)
20. Pawan ------ swimming in the sea.(be)
21. He saw that the clock -------- (stop)
22. He saw that I ------- the first prize.(win)
23. There ------ a lot of loose stones on that hillside.(be)
24. Penny ------- her class ten in 1989. (pass)
25. What ----- you -------? (do)
26. They have jjust ------ from London. (arrive)
27. He often ------ footboll at the college.
28. If he ------- hard, he will certainly succed. (work)

29 Last evening when I (meet) them in the street they (go) to the theatre

30. I (study) English for six years now.

31. Where they (go) for their holiday last year ?
32. He (leave) this place before I could meet him.
33. He usually (write) in green ink.
34. The house (be) much smaller than he (think) at first.
35. He told me his name after he (leave).
36. I don't think he will (write) before he arrives.
37. I (live) here since 1953.
38. We'll go ou when he rain.
39. If you had gone earlier. you (meet) him.
40. We were surprised to hear that see (pass) the examination at the age of fourteen.
41. He wrote to me that he (fail) in the examination.
42. I'll see yu when I (come) to Agra
43. It (be) fouteen years since I saw him.
44. We (see) that film last week.
45. I (finish) the book befoe my next bithday.
46. He told me eveything about her after she (leave)
47. When we arrived, they (have) lunch.
48. If water freezes, it (turn) to ice.
49. It (rain) since six O' clock this morning.
50. We could have stared dinner if only John (be) there.
51. Yesterday Suresh (find) a money - bag on the road.
52. Either Mohan or Babar (have) broken these glasses.
53. He (work) hard.
54. The news (be) goood.
55. It (is/has / been) raining for two hours.
56. He (wish / wished) me good morning.
57. The train Just (leave).
58. I called at his house and (give / gave) him a lesson.
59. It (rain) since yesterday afternoon.
60. The film (start) before we arrived at the cinema.
61. Let's get the book out, The servant (succed) in opening the cupboard.

62. If I (be) rich. I would be more respected.
63. Her husband (smoke) a lot now a days.
64. In 1948 I (study) English for seven years.
65. Narain (go) to see his parents every month last year.
66. When she (sing) a beautiful song, somebody knocked at the door three times.
67. India (win) the trophy twice so for.
69. We have gone to live with our house (repair) at the mount.
70. I'll never (travel) fast.
71. There (were/ was) much damage done to crops.
72. He (like) bread and butter for his breakfast.
73. The train (leave) before we reached the station.
74. I (see) the picture yesterday.
75. He (be) here since morning.
76. If I dropped this challk, it (break).
77. hen Millton entered College, he (read) most of the Greek Latin poets.
78. We can go now, I (finish) my work.
79. If you speak one word, you (be) sorry.
80. He (leave) as I came in.
81. The child (cry) because it cannot nfind its mother.
82. When we set out early this morning, the Sun (shine)
83. It was very dark early this morning but the Sun (shine) now.
84. His habit of (say) everything twice made her enjoy.
85. If dinner is not ready, I (go) without it.
86. I feel as if my head (be) on fire.
87. She said everything (go) very well until a few weeks before.
88. I (help) you if I can.
89. If it (rain) I shall stay at home.
90. Hary thought that it (not be) right to let the police know.
91. I wish I (know) his same.
92. I should not do that if I (be) you.,
93. If you (want) me to help you. why didn't you say so ?
94. It is high time you (have) a hair cut.
95. He acts as if he (know) English perfectly.

96. We (go) to the theater lasat night.
97. I never (see) show/
98. We (not live) in England for the last two years.
99. The old beggar was (bite) by a mad dog.
100. He (attend) the College everyday last week.

Exercise

Fill in the blanks with **correct form of the verbs** given in the brackets to give sense of appropriate tense:

1. I ______ Bombay six times between 1970 and 1975. *(visit)*
2. While I _____ seeds, (sow) Harry _____ up potatoes. *(dig)*
3. The girls _____ cakes all morning. *(make)*
4. My hat ______ *(blow)* off while I ______ *(cross)* the bridge.
5. When Joy Kumar _____ home *(arrive)*, his sister ___ to the wireless. *(listen)*
6. I ______ *(drop)* my watch while I _____ *(wind)* it last night.
7. She _____ letters all the afternoon. *(write)*
8. The sun _____ just ___ *(set)* when we ____ *(reach)* home.
9. I ____ the news an hour ago. *(hear)*
10. India _____ independent in 1947. *(become)*
11. My son _____ two prizes at School last term. *(win)*
12. Large crowds _____ *(wait)* at the aerodrome when the Prime Minister ___ .*(arrive)*
13. When we ____ *(set)* out this morning the sun _____(shine).
14. She _____ *(cut)* her finger while the ____ *(butter)* on the bread. .(spread)

❐ ❐ ❐

Exercise on Perfect Tenses

Exercise

Choose the correct verb form those in brackets:

1. He thanked me for what I _____. (have done, had done, have been doing)

2. I ______ a strange noise. (hear, am hearing, have been hearing)

3. I _____ him for a long time. (know, have known, am knowing)

4. We _____ English for five years. (study, am studying, have been studying)

5. Don't disturb me. I ____ my homework. (do, did, am doing)

6. Abdul ____ to be a doctor. (wants, wanting, is wanting)

7. I ____ forty next birthday. (am, shall be, have been)

8. If you _____ at once, you will arrive by six o'clock. (start, started, will start)

9. He ______ out five minutes ago. (has gone, had gone, went)

10. When he lived in Hyderabad, he _____ to the cinema once a week. (goes, went, was going)

11. The baby ____ all morning. (cries, is crying, has been crying)

12. She ____ in the concert tomorrow evening. (is playing, has played, has been playing)

13. I ____ Kumar this week. (haven't seen, didn't see, am not seeing)

14. This paper ____ twice weekly. (is appearing, appears)

15. By this time next time next year Prakash _____ his University degree. (takes, will take, will have taken)

❐ ❐ ❐

Four Forms of Verbs

FOUR FORMS OF THE VERB

Group (1)Strong Verb

1.	abide	abiding	abode	abode
2.	arise	arising	arose	arisen
3.	befall	befalling	befell	befallen
4.	beat	beating	beat	beaten
5.	bear	bearing	bore	borne
6.	become	becoming	became	become
7.	beget	begetting	begot	begotten
8.	begin	beginning	began	begun
9.	behold	beholding	beheld	beheld
10.	bespeak	bespeaking	bespoke	bespoken
11.	bestride	bestriding	bestrode	bestridden
12.	bid	biddng	bade	bidden
13.	bind	binding	bound	bound
14.	blow	blowing	blew	blown
15.	break	breaking	broke	broken
16.	cleave	cleaving	clove	cloven
17.	cling	clinging	clung	clung
18.	come	coming	came	come
19.	dig	digging	dug	dug
20.	do	doing	did	done
21.	draw	drawing	drew	drawn
22.	drink	drinking	drank	drunk
23.	drive	driving	drove	driven
24.	eat	eating	ate	eaten
25.	fall	falling	fell	fallen
26.	feed	feeding	fed	fed
27.	fling	flinging	flung	flung
28.	find	finding	found	found
29.	fly	flying	flew	flown
30.	forbear	forbearing	forbore	forborne
31.	forbid	forbidding	forebode	forbidden
32.	forget	forgetting	forgot	forgotten
33.	forgive	forgiving	forgave	forgiven
34.	forsake	forsaking	forsook	forsaken
35.	forswear	forswearing	forswore	forsworn

36.	freeze	freezing	froze	frozen
37.	get	getting	got	gotten
38.	give	giving	gave	given
39.	grind	grinding	ground	ground
40.	grow	growing	grew	grown
41.	hang	hanging	hung	hung
42.	hold	holding	held	held
43.	know	knowing	knew	known
44.	ride	riding	rode	ridden
45.	ring	ringing	rang	rung
46.	run	running	ran	run
47.	see	seeing	saw	seen
48.	shine	shining	shone	shone
49.	shoot	shooting	shot	shot
50.	shrink	shrinking	shrank	shrunk
51.	sing	singing	sang	sung
52.	sink	sinking	sank	sunk
53.	sit	sitting	sat	sat
54.	slay	slaying	slew	slain
55.	speak	speaking	spoke	spoken
56.	spit	spitting	spat	spat
57.	spring	springing	sprang	sprung
58.	steal	stealing	stole	stolen
59.	stick	sticking	stuck	stuck
60.	sting	stinging	stung	stung
61.	stride	striding	strode	stridden
62.	swear	swearing	swore	sworn
63.	swim	swimming	swam	swum
64.	swing	swinging	swung	swung
65.	take	taking	took	taken
66.	tear	tearing	tore	torn
67.	throw	throwing	threw	thrown
68.	tread	treading	trod	trodden
69.	wear	wearing	wore	worn
70.	weave	weaving	wove	woven
71.	win	winning	won	won
72.	wind	winding	wound	wound
73.	write	writing	wrote	written

Group (2) Weak Verbs

74.	abuse	abusing	abused	abused
75.	accuse	accusing	accused	accused
76.	act	acting	acted	acted
77.	advise	advising	advised	advised
78.	allow	allowing	allowed	allowed
79.	answer	answering	answered	answered
80.	appear	appearing	appeared	appeared
81.	appoint	appointing	appointed	appointed
82.	arrest	arresting	arrested	arrested
83.	arrive	arriving	arrived	arrived
84.	ask	asking	asked	asked
85.	bathe	bathing	bathed	bathed
86.	beg	begging	begged	begged
87.	believe	believing	believed	believed
88.	benefit	benefiting	benefited	benefited
89.	boast	boasting	boasted	boasted
90.	boil	boiling	boiled	boiled
91.	borrow	borrowing	borrowed	borrowed
92.	bury	burying	buried	buried
93.	buy	buying	bought	bought
94.	build	building	built	built
95.	call	calling	called	called
96.	capture	capturing	captured	captured
97.	catch	catching	caught	caught
98.	change	changing	changed	changed
99.	collect	collecting	collected	collected
100.	copy	copying	copied	copied
101.	carry	carrying	carried	carried
102.	clear	clearing	cleared	cleared
103.	creep	creeping	crept	crept
104.	climb	climbing	climbed	climbed
105.	clothe	clothing	clothed	clothed
106.	close	closing	closed	closed
107.	cook	cooking	cooked	cooked
108.	confuse	confusing	confused	confused
109.	consult	consulting	consulted	consulted

110.	compare	comparing	compared	compared
111.	count	counting	counted	counted
112.	deal	dealing	dealt	dealt
113.	dare	daring	dared	dared
114.	decorate	decorating	decorated	decorated
115.	defeat	defeating	defeated	defeated
116.	die	dying	died	died
117.	divide	dividing	divided	divided
118.	dye	dying	dyed	dyed
119.	dip	dipping	dipped	dipped
120.	deposit	depositing	deposited	deposited
121.	depend	depending	depended	depended
122.	earn	earning	earned	earned
123.	enter	entering	entered	entered
124.	face	facing	faced	faced
125.	fail	failing	failed	failed
126.	fear	fearing	feared	feared
127.	feel	feeling	felt	felt
128.	fell	felling	felled	felled
129.	fight	fighting	fought	fought
130.	float	floating	floated	floated
131.	flow	flowing	flowed	flowed
132.	gain	gaining	gained	gained
133.	gamble	gambling	gambled	gambled
134.	grant	granting	granted	granted
135.	graze	grazing	grazed	grazed
136.	hate	hating	hated	hated
137.	have	having	had	had
138.	hear	hearing	heard	heard
139.	hire	hiring	hired	hired
140.	help	helping	helped	helped
141.	hunt	hunting	hunted	hunted
142.	invite	inviting	invited	invited
143.	join	joining	joined	joined
144.	jump	jumping	jumped	jumped
145.	keep	keeping	kept	kept
146.	kick	kicking	kicked	kicked
147.	kill	killing	killed	killed

148.	laugh	laughing	laughed	laughed
149.	learn	learning	learnt	learnt
150.	leave	leaving	left	left
151.	lend	lending	lent	lent
152.	like	liking	liked	liked
153.	lift	lifting	lifted	lifted
154.	listen	listening	listened	listened
155.	live	living	lived	lived
156.	look	looking	looked	looked
157.	love	loving	loved	loved
158.	load	loading	loaded	oaded(laden)
159.	lose	losing	lost	lost
160.	make	making	made	made
161.	mean	meaning	meant	meant
162.	melt	melting	melted	melted (molten)
163.	miss	missing	missed	missed
164.	move	moving	moved	moved
165.	marry	marrying	married	married
166.	namc	naming	namcd	named
167.	need	needing	needed	needed
168.	obey	obeying	obeyed	obeyed
169.	obtain	obtaining	obtained	obtained
170.	open	opening	opened	opened
171.	oppose	opposing	opposed	opposed
172.	order	ordering	ordered	ordered
173.	owe	owing	owed	owed
174.	pass	passing	passed	passed
175.	pack	packing	packed	packed
176.	pardon	pardoning	pardoned	pardoned
177.	pay	paying	paid	paid
178.	permit	permitting	permitted	permitted
179.	play	playing	played	played
180.	preach	preaching	preached	preached
181.	prefer	preferring	preferred	preferred
182.	praise	praising	praised	praised
183.	prevent	preventing	prevented	prevented
184.	prove	proving	proved	proved

185.	promise	promising	promised	promised
186.	pen	penning	penned	penned
187.	pull	pulling	pulled	pulled
188.	pursue	pursuing	pursued	pursued
189.	please	pleasing	pleased	pleased
190.	plunder	plundering	plundered	plundered
191.	prepare	preparing	prepared	prepared
192.	present	presenting	presented	presented
193.	punish	punishing	punished	punished
194.	push	pushing	pushed	pushed
195.	publish	publishing	published	published
196.	place	placing	placed	placed
197.	promote	promoting	promoted	promoted
198.	rain	raining	rained	rained
199.	reach	reaching	reached	reached
200.	receive	receiving	received	received
201.	refuse	refusing	refused	refused
202.	reign	reigning	reigned	reigned
203.	remember	remembering	remembered	remembered
204.	reply	replying	replied	replied
205.	resign	resigning	resigned	resigned
206.	repair	repairing	repaired	repaired
207.	rest	resting	rested	rested
208.	respect	respecting	respected	respected
209.	return	returning	returned	returned
210.	raise	riasing	raised	raised
211.	ride	riding	rode	ridden
212.	rob	robbing	robbed	robbed
213.	rub	rubbing	rubbed	rubbed
214.	revenge	revenging	revenged	revenged
215.	save	saving	saved	saved
216.	salute	saluting	saluted	saluted
217.	say	saying	said	said
218.	search	searching	searched	searched
219.	seem	seeming	seemed	seemed
220.	seek	seeking	saught	saught
221.	sell	selling	sold	sold
222.	select	selecting	selected	selected

223.	send	sending	sent	sent
224.	serve	serving	served	served
225.	sew	sewing	sewed	sewed
226.	shave	shaving	shaved	shaved
227.	shear	shearing	sheared	shorne
228.	slip	slipping	slipped	slipped
229.	sleep	sleeping	slept	slept
230.	smile	smiling	smiled	smiled
231.	solve	solving	solved	solved
232.	sow	sowing	sowed	sowed
233.	spend	spending	spent	spent
234.	spell	spelling	spelt	spelt
235.	slide	sliding	slid	slid
236.	stand	standing	stood	stood
237.	start	starting	started	started
238.	starve	starving	starved	starved
239.	stop	stopping	stopped	stopped
240.	succeed	succeeding	succeeded	succeeded
241.	suffer	suffering	suffered	suffered
242.	study	studying	studied	studied
243.	stay	staying	stayed	stayed
244.	swell	swelling	swelled	swollen
245.	sweep	sweeping	swept	swept
246.	talk	talking	talked	talked
247.	tease	teasing	teased	teased
248.	tell	telling	told	told
249.	teach	teaching	taught	taught
250.	thank	thanking	thanked	thanked
251.	tied	tying	tied	tied
252.	think	thinking	thought	thought
253.	tire	tiring	tired	tired
254.	touch	touching	touched	touched
255.	trouble	troubling	troubled	troubled
256.	travel	travelling	travelled	travelled
257.	treat	treating	treated	treated
258.	trust	trusting	trusted	trusted
259.	try	trying	tried	tried
260.	unite	uniting	united	united

261.	wait	waiting	waited	waited
262.	walk	walking	walked	walked
263.	wash	washing	washed	washed
264.	want	wanting	wanted	wanted
265.	watch	watching	watched	watched
266.	wave	waving	waved	waved
267.	weep	weeping	wept	wept
268.	wish	wishing	wished	wished
269.	whistle	whistling	whistled	whistled
270.	work	working	worked	worked
271.	wound	wounding	wounded	wounded
272.	yield	yielding	yielded	yielded

Group-3

Verbs which have same present, past and past participle forms

273.	bet	betting	bet	bet
274.	bid	bidding	bid	bid
275.	burst	bursting	burst	burst
276.	cast	casting	cast	cast
277.	cost	costing	cost	cost
278.	cut	cutting	cut	cut
279.	hit	hitting	hit	hit
280.	hurt	hurting	hurt	hurt
281.	let	letting	let	let
282.	put	putting	put	put
283.	read	reading	read	read
284.	rid	ridding	rid	ridden
285.	set	setting	set	set
286.	shed	shedding	shed	shed
287.	shut	shutting	shut	shut
288.	spread	spreading	spread	spread
289.	split	splitting	split	split
290.	thrust	thrusting	thrust	thrust

❑ ❑ ❑

Index

SECTION 1

❒ ❒ ❒